Get a Job Without Going Crazy

3RD EDITION

Donna L. Shannon

Personal Touch Career Services

Westminster, CO

Personal Touch Career Services Publishing

8120 Sheridan Blvd, Suite A101

Westminster, CO 80003

https://personaltouchcareerservices.com/

720-452-3400

Get a Job Without Going Crazy/Donna L. Shannon —3rd ed.

ISBN 978-1-7312821-6-3

To Ryan

Who puts up with my insanity.

Contents

You've got to trust your instinct
And let go of regret
You've got to bet on yourself now star
'Cause that's your best bet

−311, "All Mixed Up"

1

Foreword: Look Out for Quicksand

CHANCES ARE, you probably haven't received much formal training in job searching. If you are lucky, your college may have held some classes or workshops. Similarly, you may have been seeking advice online, only to find many conflicting approaches.

How is a job seeker supposed to put a real job search strategy into play?

Fear not, gentle job hunter. As Socrates said, "True knowledge exists in knowing that you know nothing."

The fact is that the modern job search continues to evolve, requiring a fluid strategy that considers the firm bedrock of HR recruitment practices while adjusting for the shifting sands of emerging technology and trends. More than ever, job seekers need to be bold, creative, tenacious, and determined while not breaking too many rules that would annoy HR.

Most people start their job search by revising their resume and then hunting up positions on the common employment sites like Indeed.com, LinkedIn.com, ZipRecruiter.com, or even the old standards, CareerBuilder.com and Monster.com. Once viable jobs are found, they go through the motions of filling out the applications.

And then they wait.

Unfortunately, this is the worst way to try to land a job. Just like stepping into quicksand, job seekers are getting sucked down by slow, ponderous procedures that drain away their time. To make matters worse, they are fighting to be found among all the other candidates who are similarly being drawn down the ever-constricting funnel. At the end, very few of these resumes and applications are seen by human beings, because the screening computers and emerging AI technologies filter out candidates by impassive – and restrictive – keywords, education requirements, and undesirable experience.

Fortunately, there are some proven strategies to escape quicksand that are just as relevant for the job search:

1. **Drop heavy items** – or – drop those ponderous procedures that don't work.

2. **Move horizontally** – or – don't be scared to reach out to the hiring managers directly.

3. **Lay back** – or – look for unconventional solutions to common problems that may not be intuitive on the first glance.

4. **Take your time** – or – be sure to do things right the first time. You usually only get one shot at an opportunity, so don't waste your efforts by rushing and causing simple mistakes.

During the course of this book, I will show you practical strategies to generate more interviews and survive the screening process. However, it is up to you to do the work. At first, it may feel awkward and uncomfortable to reach out to managers or strategically build your network. Just keep in mind that everything gets easier with practice. If you can push through the self-conscious early phases of your job search, you will notice that it will get easier. Even better, you will start to recognize the quicksand BEFORE you step into it!

Chapter 1: What Really Happens in The HR Department

IN THE QUIET HUMAN RESOURCES DEPARTMENT, a lone figure works at her desk. As she pores over a stack of resumes, the HR Director hopes to find that perfect candidate, the one who not only meets every criterion, but also has the "perfect spark," that inexplicable quality that will take the company to the next level. She sighs as she lifts the next resume off the paper mountain. She reads carefully, weighing the merits of each candidate before setting their application aside. Her tired eyes fall on the next cover letter, low expectations written all over her face.

Her pulse quickens as she reads with disbelief – this could be the one! The experience sketched out in the letter is a perfect match for the company's needs. Eagerly, she flips to the resume: it is a home run! The perfect skill set, the perfect background, the perfect degree. She can't wait another moment to talk to this candidate. She must snatch him up before another company does.

Her hands fly to the phone. She dials nervously – what if you aren't there? What if you are interviewing somewhere else right now? She draws a tight breath while the phone rings once, then twice... Her heart skips a beat as you answer the phone. Now it is only a matter of going through the formalities of the interview before they can offer you the job of your dreams.

Did you enjoy that story? Good. Because that is never going to happen. Now that the fantasy is over with, let's discuss what the HR department is really like.

The truth is that most HR departments receive a deluge of candidates every day, far more than they could ever hope to read with any great depth or understanding. In order to process the mountain of resumes, every single company – big or small – will create simple tricks to screen candidates. You have probably heard some of these already, such as "your resume will only be read for 10 seconds." Many of these rumors are true, but it is important to understand why to get through the system.

So, like it or not, here is the ugly truth:

HR Departments Must Reduce the Candidate Field by Up To 95% – Or More.

The HR department is not your buddy, looking for the perfect job for you; it is their job to CUT YOU. The survivors of this ordeal are considered the top candidates. However, because of the screening process itself, these people might not be the most qualified candidates. They are just the ones who survived the screening process the best, which could have been the result of some job seeker tricks.

If you don't want to be a qualified casualty, learn the screening process.

HR Will Always Assume Against You.

As far as HR is concerned, if something is not on your resume, it does not exist. Therefore, it is necessary to put what may be considered very basic information on the resume. A classic example is Microsoft (MS) Office. Over the years, I have reviewed literally thousands of resumes. Every time I see that MS Office is not listed, I ask the job seeker why they left it off.

"Well," they say, "I thought it was pretty much a given that everybody knows Microsoft Office."

Not true, actually. HR certainly won't see it that way. If they must make any assumptions about a candidate's qualifications, education, skills, experience, or career focus, they will always assume the worst. After all, that is an easy cut for them.

The Average Amount of Time Spent Reading a Resume the First Time Is Less Than 10 Seconds.

HR professionals do not spend time poring over the details in your resume. They are taking a quick look to see if you have the minimum skills and/or experience they want. If HR can't see your value in 10 seconds or less, your resume is rejected.

Very few people are excited about reading through a stack of resumes. And who can blame them? Most resumes are boring, monotonous, poorly written, or filled with fluffy phrases or outright bragging. That's why...

Lower-Level HR Employees Do the Initial Screening.

It is tedious to go through a stack of resumes. So, HR managers make the assistants do the first layer of cuts. That is, if you are lucky enough to get an actual human being at all. These screeners follow very literal and specific qualifications to screen the resumes. Sometimes they may not understand that certain skills are related. For example, HR people frequently must screen IT resumes; however, very few of them really understand which software programs derivatives or related versions are. If your resume is not using the right key terms or jargon, you probably will be cut, no matter how qualified you are. Not only that, the screeners have very little oversight on their work. Nobody is checking to see if you got cut or not – unless you are networking with managers at the company.

Computers Are Screening You Out.

Ah, the dreaded Applicant Tracking System, or ATS. If you have ever filled out an online application, chances are that you are being screened by the computerized ATS. While it used to be that only the large companies could afford to use ATS, modern improvements have made ATS affordable to even small, local companies. So, why is that bad?

While entry-level HR people may lack understanding, the computers are literally looking for an exact match on the keywords. I have seen people kicked out by the computer because they didn't have a degree when, in fact, they held a relevant bachelor's degree. However, their resume said "B.S.," and the computer was looking for "Bachelor of Science."

B.S., indeed.

The ATS is brutal, literal, and unforgiving. Worse, it stands between you and any chance that a human being will read your resume and grant you an interview.

You Need A 50 – 70% Keyword Match to Get Past the Screeners.

NOTE: that is a match on KEYWORDS, not QUALIFICATIONS! This includes both smart and stupid keywords. A smart keyword is one that relates to the actual functions of your job, such as "consultative sales process, negotiations, and account management" for a sales person. The stupid keywords are the clichés that we all hate, such as "excellent communication skills" and "team player." As humans, we know these phrases don't mean much, but the computers are looking for them.

As long as HR puts these boring terms in the job description, you must have them somewhere on your resume or risk being screened out by the computers, simply because you lack the right keywords.

Job Descriptions Are Not Absolutes.

If you are getting skeptical about the screening process, it's about to get a lot worse. Sometimes the job description – that sacred document that is used to screen the candidates – isn't even an accurate assessment of the job. How the heck did that happen?

Poor communication and interdepartmental rivalry can sometimes be the culprit, but short deadlines can get in the way as well. Usually, when getting ready to post a job, HR will send the old job description to the hiring manager. If you are lucky, the manager then carefully reads and edits the job description before sending it back to HR. If you aren't lucky, the hiring manager will tell HR to "just post the old job listing." Sometimes the company doesn't have a very collaborative culture, which can lead to misunderstandings between the departments on what qualifications and experience are really needed for the job. Regardless of the process, hiring managers and HR professionals do not spend hours constructing the perfect job description.

They throw it together quickly and according to the company's approved format.

Ever hear the statement; "if you don't have all of the qualifications, apply anyway?" That is true! And here's why...

HR frequently adds some things to the job description to deter lower-level candidates. The hiring manager may not care about these standards at all. For example, when I did recruiting, I would always ask the hiring manager if a degree was required for the job. Many times, I heard, "it doesn't matter, so long as they can do the job." However, I still added "Bachelor's degree preferred," just because I knew that I would receive less candidates.

HR Departments Won't Read Everything You Send Them.

This fact is often a shock for many job seekers. One common misconception is that a strong cover letter can overcome a weak resume, or vice versa. In fact, HR now cares less about the cover letter than ever before.

In October 2017, my company, the Personal Touch Career Services, did a survey of HR professionals in the Denver area. We found that only 50% of recruiters cared about the cover letter. In fact, 40% of them do not even accept cover letters on their online applications. These are not small companies; it includes large international corporations such as Lockheed Martin.

Cover letters are not a waste of time. The keywords within them still do count. Plus, a targeted cover letter sent to the hiring manager can do wonders to open doors. But they must be very specific to the company's needs, and not about what you want. If you can show the managers that you can benefit their bottom line or solve nagging problems, they will definitely be more interested in talking to you.

On the flip side, we know that social media continues to grow in the recruitment space...

90% Of Recruiters Will Look at Your LinkedIn Profile.

LinkedIn tells the rest of your story beyond your resume. This is why 90% of recruiters use it to look at candidates before they are called in for an interview (LinkedIn, 2016). Your LinkedIn profile needs to be complete, robust, and keyword-optimized to attract recruiters and managers alike.

Employers Won't Hire the Perfect Candidate. They Hire the Closest Match at the Right Price.

The right price does not mean the cheapest candidate. They are looking for someone who matches the most critical skills and experience while staying within a given budget.

With all this working against you, the job search may seem more difficult than ever. However, once you understand the rules, you can make them work for you – and know when to break them. In the upcoming chapters, we'll cover the specific techniques you'll need to get past the guard dogs.

Remember, just like escaping quicksand, sometimes we need to stop struggling and take the non-intuitive steps to make real progress.

Chapter 2: Finding A Job You Love

SURE, EVERYBODY WANTS TO FIND A GOOD JOB. But what about finding one that you really love? Yes, it really is possible, if you are willing to put in the effort to make it happen. Let me give you my personal story....

When I was a kid, I wanted to be an on-air DJ. Not just any DJ, but specifically a wacky morning DJ on the radio. I would record comedy bits on a tape recorder at home, mixed to cassette along with top rock songs and Weird Al Yankovic parodies. Now, remember, this was back in the 1980s, so there was no internet to broadcast my dubious humor attempts, but my stuffed animals thought I was great.

By the time I hit high school, I was a top student with solid grades and active in the theatre program. It seemed like a shoo-in that I could go to pretty much any college that I wanted. However, that crazy kid's ambition still had not gone away. One day, I met with my guidance counselor to plan out the rest of my life.

"I want to be a radio DJ," I proudly proclaimed.

My counselor looked at me with a blank stare, blinked a few times, and said, "I have no idea on how to make that happen." I really don't remember the rest of the conversation after that, but I am sure he was trying to push more reasonable career paths on me. (By the way, the typical path is that you attend a school with an on-campus radio station and major in Communications, but I didn't find that out until 10 years later.)

In fact, my entire college plans were set back by five years, as I became pregnant and married when I was 17, in that order specifically. I did get my diploma from my original high school, finishing my classes six months early. I even acted in the school play when I was seven months pregnant; we performed "David and Lisa," which is about teenagers in a mental institution. The pregnancy certainly added a lot to my character, to say the least. Once high school ended, I stayed home with the kids for five years, ending up with three children that I loved dearly, even though I was far from a "June Cleaver" mom. Think more like "Malcolm in the Middle" with more Metallica.

Yet, those crazy music industry dreams still didn't quite die.

In 1992, I discovered the Art Institute of Colorado's video production/audio engineering/music business management program. After earning an Associates of Applied Science in 1994, I began searching for my first job in radio. By that time, I was finalizing my divorce and secured a glamorous part-time job in the print shop of Office Depot. Scouring through the want ads – such things were printed in the Sunday newspaper back then – I kept my eye open for anything in broadcasting. Finally, my luck paid off: Clear Channel Broadcasting in Denver was looking for a part-time Mail Room Jockey. Not only was this radio, they held and operated my absolute top choice radio station, the heavy metal/hard rock KBPI-FM. While the job was technically in the business office that handled all eight stations Clear Channel owned in the Denver market, I saw ways to use this toehold to leverage this into an on-air role.

Since the job was only part-time, I retained my job at the print shop. However, there was a snag with that: as a single mom with three kids under 7 years old, I was receiving certain government assistance benefits, including a limited welfare check. The second job put me $20 a month over the financial limit to receive welfare, although I did retain what helped the most: child care assistance and Medicaid for the kids. While challenging, I didn't have a problem with this, as I didn't like getting a government check in the first place. My sister, on the other hand, said I was stupid and that I should quit the jobs and just "soak the government for as much as I can." However, I didn't want to live a life on handouts. I wanted to meet very specific career goals, even if they were crazy.

For the next three years, I worked my way up in Clear Channel's business office, first becoming full time and later moving into the Accounts Receivable role before becoming the Assistant to the Controller in 1997. Once I moved into a salaried rather than an hourly role, I petitioned our HR department to allow me to take a new hourly role without incurring overtime while keeping my full-time day job in the business office. Why would I do this? Well, the AM stations were looking for Technical Producers and Board Operators for the overnight weekend shifts. Knowing that I had to improve my technical skills before I could make a bid for an air staff job at KBPI, I knew that any studio time was necessary to brush up on my rusty training from school. Now, I will readily admit that, at first, I really sucked. It had been three years since I had operated professional quality audio equipment, a deficiency that was glaringly obvious. However, rather than firing me, the AM stations retrained me and allowed me to continue.

Flash forward another year. KBPI's Morning Show, Kerry & Kerns, was looking for a Morning Show Producer. Finally, this was the opportunity that I had been working for. I went through the interviews and an audition process. While I am certain that I wasn't the best candidate, I think my passion, dedication, and just plain unfailing belief that I could do the job won it for me.

At the time, both general managers from the AM and FM sides of the business said they had never seen someone make a move from the business office to producing a major-market morning show in their 15 years of experience. It was a real 90-degree career turn!

Of course, I sucked at first. Definitely a large learning curve, but I adapted. I even found out that my team was teased about hiring an accountant to be their producer. In the end, they defended my abilities, as few other producers in their past experience had been as organized with essentials like securing press credentials, scheduling interviews, or tracking files and materials. Don't get me wrong – I still screwed up a LOT, including one incident that caused me to be banished to the graveyard shift for four months and not being allowed to talk on the air. Nevertheless, I continued to be given second chances and opportunities to turn my performance around.

In the end, personal issues took me away from the radio station almost a year after making it to an air staff role. It was both an exhilarating and challenging time in my life, a time that would not have been possible without the support of my extended family and of Mike, my husband who I married while I was part of the morning show. When it was all said and done, I can honestly say that I mostly loved my experiences, although I wished I had handled some things differently. But that is real life, even for a dream job. Nothing is exactly how we picture it and we need to make sure that the sacrifices we choose to obtain it are worth the cost.

It took me about a year of working temporary jobs and sorting out my personal issues after that to decide what I really wanted to be when I grew up – this time, "for real." I concluded that I actually loved the business side of the broadcasting environment, and I secured a job as the HR Recruiter/Accountant for the local PBS TV station in Denver, Rocky Mountain PBS Channel 6.

Working at Channel 6 directly led to what would become my true life-long mission and personal calling: to help job seekers by educating them in how real-world hiring practices work. Since 2004, I have been teaching people how to land a job that they love – yet another 90-degree turn that allowed me to follow my passions while capitalizing on my past experience, education, and strengths.

So why am I telling you all of this?

Because I am not asking you to do anything that I have not done myself – more than once. It IS possible to get the job of your dreams, find your path, take new directions, and change your mind at any time. And I am going to tell you exactly how to do it.

Three Keys to Finding That Job You Love

Before we start talking about searching up jobs online or hunting down ideal companies that have drawn your attention, let's establish some clear parameters that will lead to getting a job that you actually love.

Ultimately, it comes down to three things:

1. Be Yourself
2. Be Honest
3. Be Aware

Be Yourself

If you really want a job that you love, you need to be willing to take the biggest risk of all: be yourself. Of course, you want to present the best version of yourself in your materials like your resume or LinkedIn profile, but in the end, if you are just putting up a false front to fit into a corporate structure, it won't work for the long term.

As a former corporate recruiter, I absolutely hated it when a job candidate told me what they thought I wanted to hear in the interview. In modern hiring, this is even more infuriating. Employers want to hire someone who is a good fit for their corporate culture, but if the job seeker is putting up a front, they really can't tell what they are getting.

So, who are you?

Before you pull out your dream journal and start making a vision board, let's keep this focused on your work life. I'm not talking about job titles or college degrees either. Let's really break it down into what you really enjoy about your work versus the parts that aren't so appealing.

Love, It, Like It, Live with It, Or Loathe It: The 4 Ls

For this exercise, think back over your career. We are going to explore not just the jobs themselves, but what you were doing in each position – the actual duties and responsibilities that filled your days.

Under each one of the columns, sort these actions by the Four Ls: did you love it, like it, live with it or loathe it? Give each of the duties real consideration, even if they were performed at different jobs. What did you really love to do? Is there something that you would gladly do, even if you didn't get paid for it? Are there aspects of your work that you enjoy, but it's not your be-all, end-all passion in life? How about duties that you can live with, if they are a requirement for the job? Finally, are there things that you absolutely loathed, that set your teeth on edge? Things that you would absolutely give anything to not have to do at all?

Love It	Like It	Live With It	Loathe It
I would happily do more of this..	I enjoy this..	I can do this if it is essential to the job...	I would give anything to not have to...

Now, as grown-ups, we realize that there are times when we must do things that we don't necessarily enjoy. There is a reason why it is called "work." However, the goal is to move into a role where you get to do enough of the things that you Love and Like that it makes the other side of the spectrum less intolerable.

Example: The 4 Ls
In this following example, I was working with a new college graduate who had a degree in Sports Marketing and Management. He really wanted to get involved with a major sports team in our market, ideally in the back office. After doing some brainstorming on the phone, I told him about Kroenke Sports – owners of the Denver Nuggets,

Colorado Avalanche, and the Colorado Mammoth Lacrosse teams –
and their sales internship program in Denver. Basically, the fledgling
inside sales people were on the phone constantly for three months,
trying to gain interest in the season ticket packages. At the end of
three months, whoever met or exceeded the minimum sales targets
were moved into a full account executive role. Neat, right? Except for
when we went over his 4 Ls together, and the results looked like this:

Love It	Like It	Live With It	Loathe It
I would happily do more of this..	I enjoy this..	I can do this if it is essential to the job...	I would give anything to not have to...
Physical therapy for athletes Project Management Being creative Sports of all types Product gamification and promotion	Social media campaigns Content development Graphic arts Physical fitness programs Traking performance metrics Negotiations Vendor Management	Attending large networking events Giving presentations	Cold calling Hard sales Meet set quotas Prospecting Lead generation

Obviously, EVERYTHING that he hated is exactly what a salesman
does all day long! While the sales internship may have given him a
toehold in the Kroenke organization, it would have been a miserable
failure and, worse, created a bad track record with a potential employer.

After evaluating his Four Ls and looking at his background, experience, skills, and degree, his real path became more apparent. What
he really wanted to do was the physical therapy aspect for

professional athletes – a variation of his career that he held while attending school – or to move into the promotional department for a sports team, working on such projects as in-game promotions, graphics, community programs, and other ways to help foster goodwill between the team and the community at large.

So, what was the problem?

Too many people told him those jobs were too rare, so he should focus on sales because those jobs were "easy to get." Rather than just going after the low-hanging fruit, we developed a more tactical plan that built on his strengths, got him practical experience in related fields or companies, and identified ways to get involved with the team's charitable foundation while watching for those potential job openings. Even if he didn't land a job with the Denver Broncos or the Avalanche, we discovered TONS of local sports organizations that worked with athletes of all levels, from teams to merchandisers and fitness companies to athletic gear manufacturers.

THIS is why it is important to be yourself. Don't squeeze into a role that you know is a bad fit that is probably doomed to fail. I am all for putting up with some discomfort if it leads to your long-term goal but taking a job you hate will not work. It will kill your passion.

One more thing: don't forget about the related industries or jobs to your passion. All told, I spent eight years in broadcasting, between Clear Channel and Rocky Mountain PBS. In the end, the job at the television station was more rewarding. Had I kept tunnel vision that only on-air radio jobs were my career goal, I would have missed out on becoming a career coach. Consider this too: even personality tests aren't absolutes, as they require interpretation. My tests said I should be a teacher. Obviously, I'm not going back to school to teach elementary school kids. But one of the things I love the most about my career now is teaching job seekers how to find a job. With that 90-degree turn interpretation, everything I do starts to make sense.

Be Honest

The second key to landing a job you love is being honest. Being honest applies to many levels. Of course, you must be honest with employers

– but not TOO honest, of course! Job searching is like marketing, so while you do need to put your best foot forward and showcase your best talents, you want to downplay the negatives. I will dive into those strategies throughout this book, but first, let's do some self-evaluation.

When considering any career move, you need to make an honest assessment of your skills, talents, and education to make sure you have the right tools to move into that next job. This should be a personal inventory of both your strengths and deficiencies, along with the challenges that stand in your way of meeting your goals. Once the complete assessment is done, you can find your best-selling points and present them to any employer. Plus, you can come up with ways to address the weaknesses before you are asked about them.

Before you wildly start listing random things about yourself, pull up some sample job postings that match your target job. The more detailed they are, the better. Look at least five different ads for the same job title or type of job. Pay close attention to the Qualifications or Requirements section, especially regarding any of the technical and soft skills listed for the job. When considering your own technical skills, use these real-world job postings as a guide on what employers are really looking for. Don't get too hung up on the required education or years of experience at this time, unless it is explicitly stated that those are required for the job. Believe it or not, not having the ideal work history doesn't close the door, especially if you reach out to hiring managers directly.

For this inventory, remember that all your personal traits that will help with your job search, even if the employer isn't asking for them. These are things like perseverance, determination, creative problem solving, organization, and strategy development. If you are more extroverted, stating that you love meeting people is an advantage. If you are more introverted, your strengths lie in research, listening skills, and personal contemplation.

Finally, take note of your relevant experience and education. NOTE: look for your 90-degree turns. When I went from the business office to producing a radio morning show, all my organization skills that I learned from accounting were a huge advantage on the job. Most companies are willing to accept degrees no matter what their discipline. Similarly, the exponential growth of online, self-directed learning opportunities like www.udemy.com are definitely relevant. Remember to include those sources.

My Strengths			
Skills	Personal Traits	Job Searching Talents	Relevant Experience & Education
Specific skills as listed in the job description	Soft skills pulled from the job description	My personal traits that give me an advantage	Direct or indirect experience & education that makes me ideal for the job

What Is Your Greatest Weakness?

I know what you are thinking: "Why did she put that cheesy interview question in here?"

Yes, you are right – that is a cheesy interview question. But when you are looking at making a career shift, you can use it as a personal reflection tool. While you would never use this exercise to answer the interview question, it is important to recognize your weakness – and, more importantly, discuss how to overcome it.

First of all, let's dive into those technical skills. Just as those job descriptions helped identify the strong skills you already possess, they should also reveal key areas that need to be addressed. This might mean taking some additional classes, getting certifications, or, in the most extreme cases, gaining a different degree.

For example, some time ago, I decided that I wanted to move into a Human Resources Manager role. I had the eight years of experience in HR, so I figured that this would be a no-brainer. Keep in mind that I had already been teaching job searching courses for about four years at that point. But after six months of searching, I didn't land even one management-level interview. I took a step back and analyzed several job descriptions and determined that practically every single one of them wanted a bachelor's degree specifically in HR, combine with a PHR (Professional in HR) or SPHR (Senior Professional in HR) certification. Unfortunately, I only had an Associate's in an unrelated field and no certifications.

My Weaknesses		
Skills	Education or Experience	Corrective Actions
Specific skills as listed in the job description	Missing degrees, certifications, or relevant experience	Ways to boost skills, possible education, formal or not

So, what could I do? Networking or being charming was not going to get me the job this time. They really needed that higher level of expertise and knowledge. Still determined to make the change, I went back to college to gain that degree, even though it meant a three-year plan to accomplish it. (By the way, I changed my major halfway through to Entrepreneurship to start my own business and dive deeper into my actual calling of being a career coach, earning my Bachelor's in 2012.)

Bottom line: when looking at these weaknesses, don't get down on yourself. Skills can be learned. Certifications can be obtained. Networking with managers can open doors that HR shut. If you are serious – REALLY SERIOUS – about making the career change, use this assessment as the first step to clearly identify what you need to add to be successful.

Be Aware

The final key to landing a job you love is to be aware. From paying attention to what is going on in your local market to looking for subtle red flags and clues during an interview, being aware will let you find hidden gems while avoiding horrible situations.

A lot of this book deals with being aware throughout the job search process in its entirety. Knowing how the HR department works will give you an advantage in surviving the screening process. Realizing that it is acceptable to reach out to hiring managers can earn you interviews, even when HR cut you. Identifying target companies will help you find jobs in the elusive hidden job market. Expanding your network in both live and online platforms will lead to more opportunities.

But before we dive into all of that, there is another thing that we need to be aware of: how the employers perceive us. Then, and only then, we can develop strategies to overcome any potential objections.

Dealing with Discrepancies

You may have less-than-ideal situations in your past or current employment situations. How do you deal with issues such as gaps in your employment, switching fields, or a lack of experience?

The first thing to change is your attitude. Conducting an empowered job search means reconciling your feelings about the past.

Don't ignore an issue and then hope it won't be addressed in the interview. If you acknowledge the stumbling blocks beforehand, you can deal with them in an effective way. Acceptance is the answer.

HR people are trained to spot the discrepancies in a resume. However, that does not mean a ripple in your experience will kill your chances. It IS possible to get HR and hiring managers beyond the knee-jerk reaction of cutting any candidate that has a less-than-perfect work history. To do that, you need to look at the problem from the employers' point of view. What are their objections or concerns? If you can address the objection right from the start, you can move past it.

Three Steps to Reframing A Discrepancy

Every situation can be dealt with, if you have the courage to face it.

To reframe a problem, follow these crucial steps:

1. Honestly state what the issue is
2. Consider it from the employer's point-of-view
3. Discover the positive in the situation

To reframe a discrepancy, take a moment to write down what you think may be holding you back. Be honest and thorough, writing down what the real issue is. However, don't get brutal about it. It's one thing to say, "well, I have had several short-term jobs." But stating, "my work history is so full of short-term jobs, no employer will ever take a chance on me!" That's not honest; that's just brutal and fatalistic.

Next, think of this problem from the employer's point-of-view. An unstable work history makes them nervous that you will not stay for a long-term job. If you are switching industries, the employer must take a risk that you will catch on quickly. Sometimes, a job seeker may have been laid off, and the employer wants to be certain that they weren't terminated for performance issues. Whatever the case, put yourself in the employer's shoes, but don't get brutal in your reasons for being skeptical.

Finally, think about how the discrepancy could be considered a positive. Write down your answer to those objections. It needs to be clear, specific, and positive. For example, short-term jobs help you adapt quickly to new situations. Breaking into an industry means you are highly motivated to make a good impression on the job, not to mention bringing new ideas to the table. Even being laid off means that you already have valuable experience.

NOTE: this is a great exercise to do with another person, as two heads are better than one!

Dealing With Discrepancies		
The Issue	Employer's Objections	The Positive Spin

Attitude is a major factor in the job search process. A bad attitude affects confidence levels, which employers can sense like blood in the water. On the flip side, dealing with discrepancies with a positive attitude shows maturity, personal insight, and poise. Even if you were flat-out fired, an employer can value someone who has learned from the situation and is ready to move on.

Let's do one example on a discrepancy that I hear all the time: ageism. Even people in their 40s are worried about age discrimination in the workplace. However, there are many strategies to minimize this impact.

Dealing With Discrepancies: Ageism

The Issue	Employer's Objections	The Positive Spin
I am too old for the job market Employers are favoring younger workers	Experienced workers are more expensive Overqualified Not as tech-savy on latest technologies Set in their ways Wil continue to look for a better/higher paying job after we hire them	State your desired salary ranges to show you understand fair market for the role Experience is valuable in overcoming problems Prove you can learn by taking courses/classes Explore new technologies & make sure you are active on Linkedin, etc. Prove work ethic & communication skills Show commitment to company and their mission, along with excitment for the job Only list 10-15 years of experience Remove graduation date from education

Remember, the Issue and the Objection themselves may be PERCEIVED problems in your mind and may not be as prevalent as you think. This is why you need to BE AWARE of reality, and not reactionary to your own fears or concerns.

What Are You Willing to Do?

Landing a dream job or even a good job takes effort, dedication, time, and some degree of intestinal fortitude. If you are really serious about making a change, you may need to change your behaviors for a while. This is the real difference between dreams and reality: what are you willing to do to meet your goals?

For this exercise, write down simply what are you willing and not willing to do. THERE ARE NO WRONG ANSWERS, ONLY CHOICES. For example, are you willing to accept less salary for a chance to change careers – and, if so, by how much? Are you willing to go get necessary certifications to fill in a skills gap? Are you willing to attend networking events after hours, even if it takes time away from your family? Are you willing to go out of your comfort zone and approach people on LinkedIn? How far are you willing to drive every day to get to your job? How about travel, including how far and how much?

What I'm WILLING to do:	What I'm NOT WILLING to do:

Sometimes these choices are very simple, like how much time can you devote to your job search. I know one person who hates the job he's held for 15 years, but every day, when he comes home from work, he plays video games for three hours – and up to eight hours a day on the weekend. If he were willing to devote that time to his job search, he would have moved on to greener pastures long ago.

Do you want your job search to remain a dream?

If not, then make a statement – a commitment if you will – about what you are willing or not willing to do. Show this to your family and friends for their support and understanding, along with their agreement. Once you have made these choices, it is time to treat your job search like a job!

Chapter 3: "Treat Your Job Search Like A Job" - What Does That Mean?

CHANCES ARE, YOU HAVE HEARD THAT CLICHÉ BEFORE. But what does it mean? Most people assume that it relates to the number of hours they spend on their job search. They mentally commit 40 hours or more a week to their job search, but beyond looking at the jobs posted on the online sites, they aren't certain about what they are supposed to do.

Your New Employee – Yourself

Treating your job search like a job goes way beyond just structuring time to do it. In truth, you are the manager of a very small department with only one employee: yourself. If you start thinking like a manager, you can recognize that this employee has some challenges you must address:

- A poor work environment.

- No set schedules.

- Unknown performance standards.

First of all, you have a poor work environment. Unless you are already accustomed to working from home, it can be hard to instill the discipline to work diligently. Everything can be a distraction, from the beloved pets to the beloved TV.

Be prepared to carve out a workspace specifically for your job search. Just setting up a spot on the kitchen table isn't going to work. You need somewhere that the entire household understands is your thinking spot (except the cats, who won't respect your boundaries anyway.)

Even the computer itself can be a poor work environment. Have you ever gone online to "look up just one thing" and then get sucked into the news feeds or social media? Next thing you know, 20 minutes has gone by, and if you are like me, you can't even remember what you were searching for in the first place. It may be necessary to change your home landing page on your browser during your job search to cut down these distractions. Similarly, if you have desktop or phone apps that chime all the time, restrict or even – gasp! – turn them off. It's been well documented that every distraction causes you to take time to reengage mentally with the task at hand.

Second, there is the problem of lacking a set schedule. For some people, knowing their actual work hours makes it easier to be productive. When you are searching for a job, it's all on your own time. There are very few outside forces dictating deadlines or even start times. If you already have a job, it can be even more difficult to carve out time for the job search, as your evenings, weekends, and early mornings may already be filled with family or personal commitments.

If you are unemployed, there is a subtler trap that is caused by your family or friends. You may be asked to help out with special projects, especially since you have all this "free time" because you aren't working right now. Sometimes you might even sabotage yourself in this way. I have worked with clients who would rather scrub their toilets than attend a noontime networking group or search through online job ads. After all, cleaning the bathroom gives you a tangible result. Many job seekers take that bait because it actually feels productive, as opposed to job searching in a vacuum where they get very little feedback.

That brings up the 3rd challenge: unknown performance standards.

What's the biggest clue that your job search is successful? You get a job offer, right? But that's the END GAME. You need to know your key performance indicators (KPIs) throughout the search.

Key Performance Indicators (KPIs) For Job Seekers

While you may not be getting direct feedback from the employers during your search, keep in mind these KPIs and other performance standards to see how successful your job search is:

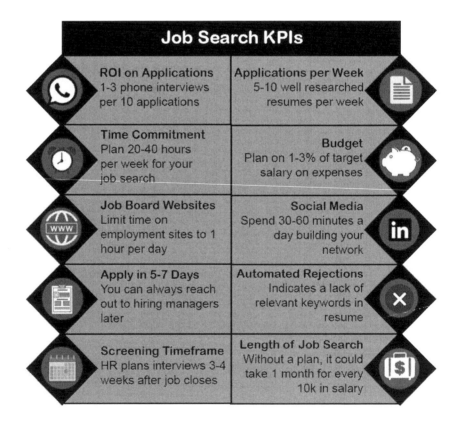

Job Search KPIs

ROI on Applications
1-3 phone interviews per 10 applications

Applications per Week
5-10 well researched resumes per week

Time Commitment
Plan 20-40 hours per week for your job search

Budget
Plan on 1-3% of target salary on expenses

Job Board Websites
Limit time on employment sites to 1 hour per day

Social Media
Spend 30-60 minutes a day building your network

Apply in 5-7 Days
You can always reach out to hiring managers later

Automated Rejections
Indicates a lack of relevant keywords in resume

Screening Timeframe
HR plans interviews 3-4 weeks after job closes

Length of Job Search
Without a plan, it could take 1 month for every 10k in salary

- You should be landing 1 to 3 phone interviews for every 10 resumes or applications that you submit.

- Plan on submitting 5 to 10 applications/resumes per week. It is more effective to do an exceptional job on a few top targets vs. applying to a large number of jobs.

- Commit 20 to 40 hours per week to your job search.

- Spend a MAXIMUM of one hour a day on the job boards like Indeed.com, ZipRecruiter.com, and others. Automate your searches on the job boards to increase your effectiveness.

- Spend at least 30 to 60 minutes a day, or more, on LinkedIn. This includes finding jobs, posting content, making comments in group discussions, connecting with recruiters, and searching for hiring managers.

- You want to apply to a position within 5 business days of the original listing date unless they state a specific closing date. Remember, you can reach out to the hiring managers a few days later but get your formal application into HR within 7 days. If more than 2 weeks has passed, contact the company to make sure the job is still open.

- If you are getting automated rejections within 24-48 hours after your application, there is something wrong with the keywords in your resume because the screening computers are kicking you out.

- If you haven't heard back from HR within 2-4 weeks, they probably are moving forward with other candidates; however, large companies or technical roles may take 2-3 months. State and federal government jobs can take 6-12 months.

- For most people, it takes 1 month of job searching per every $10,000 in salary you want. For example, if you are seeking a $100,000 job, it may take 10 months to land one. However, utilizing the strategies in this book will greatly reduce that time estimate.

- Budget at least 1-3% of your target salary for your job search expenses. This could include resume writing services, monthly LinkedIn Premium fees, exclusive websites like TheLadders.com, or potential travel.

One more thing: strong managers practice solid strategies for success. As a job seeker, the keys to being an effective manager are:

Establish clear GOALS based on what you really want. Develop a work structure based on your preferred WORK STYLE. Know your KPIs to gauge your effectiveness and increase your motivation. Implement PROVEN STRATEGIES to keep your search moving forward.

While we will definitely cover these aspects throughout this book, let's get started with a classic management tool: the job description.

Job Seeker Job Description

For most job seekers, just knowing what they should be doing on a daily basis can be a challenge. We all know the typical functions – go online, look for jobs on websites, apply to jobs – but a smart and savvy job seeker knows it takes much more than this to be effective. Just like any job, hunting for employment can be broken down into specific areas of responsibility:

Management

- Develop overall strategic plans for the job search
- Set specific, measurable, achievable, and timely goals and deadlines
- Test and find best working environment, such as time of day or location

Business Development

- Develop a list of potential or target employers
- Set up Google Alerts on target employers

- Conduct outbound calls for informational interviews at target companies
- Network at live events through associations, business groups, or job seeker groups
- Reach out to past or current employees at target companies to conduct in-depth research
- Research and contact managers at target companies
- Follow up on submissions to HR
- Build strategic alliances with recruiters and other job seekers
- Gain referrals/recommendations from past clients, managers and fellow employees
- Create and update a database system to track progress on job search
- Foster social media relationships
- Join social media groups specific to your location, industry, and interests
- Find and apply to jobs on job boards such as Indeed.com, Career-Builder, etc.
- Search LinkedIn Groups for hidden job postings
- Build social media connections with recruiters

Marketing

- Create professional, perfect resumes with relevant keywords for target jobs
- Write custom cover letters for jobs, both for HR and for specific hiring managers
- Upload a dynamic, keyword-rich LinkedIn profile with a high-quality photograph
- Manage or clean up all social media accounts
- Share meaningful content on LinkedIn, especially to Groups
- Practice interviewing techniques

- Evaluate your wardrobe to search for potential interview outfits
- Create presentations for interviews (if requested)

Finance and Accounting

- Set a budget for the job search (typically 3-7% of target salary. Typical expenses include resume services, classes, networking events, food/treats for informational interviews, travel expenses, etc.)
- Track expenses to use as tax deductions
- Find free or affordable fun things to do around town (there's more to life than just job searching)

Human Resources

- Do nice things for your network to stay in their good graces
- Keep track of 401(k)/IRA from previous employers

IT and Technical

- Ensure proper operation of all equipment, internet connections and on-location IT operations
- Conduct data backups
- Catalog warranty information

Administrative

- Calendar management
- Data entry, inbound/outbound mail
- Create email lists to send monthly updates to friends, family, and recruiters
- Generate materials for interviews, including printing high-quality resumes, samples of work, and copies of awards or letters of recommendation
- Organize networking contact follow-ups
- Manage office supplies

- Record any necessary documentation for governmental agencies, including Unemployment or Workforce Investment Act (WIA) grants

The Business of Your Business

In addition to these responsibilities, remember to stay sharp professionally. This may mean taking classes in the latest software or creating mock projects in your area of expertise. Volunteer experience can be valuable, especially if you can do something related to your field or helps build your network.

The Four Work Styles: Goals, Schedules, Deadlines, and Lists

Has anyone ever told you that you need goals to be successful? I know that, as a business owner, I would hear this all the time. However, the problem was I am not a typical goal-driven person. I know that may seem strange, considering what you know about my work history. While I can dream up creative ways to land interesting jobs, I truly struggle when addressing the commonplace, boots-on-the-ground, metrics-driven goals. This includes setting monthly sales revenue targets or quantifying other results, such as making 50 cold calls in a week. While I would start with good intentions, the fact is that I would run away – at least mentally – from the tasks that I found most unpleasant, such as those dreaded cold calls. By the time Friday afternoon rolled around, I would make a half-hearted attempt to pick up the phone and call strangers. Of course, it didn't work, AND I didn't meet the goal of 50 calls. I would feel like such a failure.

Then I realized something. Not everybody is motivated by goals. Even better, there is nothing wrong with that. Instead, I am driven by different motivations, which is reflected in my personal working style. Once I recognized my personal work style and played to my strengths, I can actually meet and exceed the previously daunting goals that, in the end, were holding me back.

If you are like many job seekers, you probably can relate to the challenges with trying to set goals and then struggle to meet them –

not to mention the feeling of defeat when they aren't met for any number of reasons. Instead, I want to you to explore these four different work styles or any combinations that help you complete your job search. Specifically, the four work styles are Goals, Schedules, Deadlines, and Lists.

Building A Rewards System

It's no secret that job seeking is a tough business. One of the worst parts is the constant rejection or "radio silence" from the HR departments. Because job seekers get very little positive feedback, you need to build in the positive reinforcement along the way – after all, that's what a responsible manager does!

When you build a strategy that favors your preferred work style, it naturally creates little successes that keep you going. For example, a goal-driven person would gain a sense of achievement from making those 20 tough calls. Someone who finds comfort in schedules can mark out time on their calendar for calls. A person focused on deadlines would thrive under the pressure of knowing the due date. Finally, our list maker's reward is literally crossing that pesky item off the to-do list.

Remember to build in your rewards. They are essential not only for your motivation, but also for your self-esteem and mental health as well.

Goals:

Goals is probably the most recognized of all the work styles. People who are goal-driven are the most effective when they are striving to meet a certain target. The more specific the goals are, the better. In fact, the SMART acronym for goals is one of the cornerstones of business.

SMART goals are Specific, Measurable, Attainable, Realistic, and Timely:

Specific: Clearly state the specific things you want to accomplish, or be left feeling direction less.

Measurable: Track contacts, number of applications you submitted, etc to keep goals measurable.

Attainable: Stay motivated and avoid getting overwhelmed with attainable, but challenging, goals.

Realistic: A realistic goal helps you stay focused while taking the length of the process in to account.

Timely: A sense of urgency will keep you from procrastinating and missing out on opportunities.

Some examples of SMART goals for a job search could be:

- I will research 10 companies this week.

- I will apply to 3 jobs today.

- I will finish my LinkedIn profile to an Expert level by Tuesday.

The trick is to meet ALL the criteria for the SMART goals. Being too vague or unrealistic will de-motivate you or leave you floundering, not sure what your next move should be. Always think about how you can break down the job searching process into smaller, attainable goals to give you a sense of accomplishment once they are reached.

Schedules

Someone who favors schedules benefits from having a set calendar, with a clear plan for the day or the week. Schedulers can sometimes struggle with the job search, as there are few hard-and-fast appointments set in stone, especially if they are unemployed. The big trick here is to create your own schedule and then perform it consistently until it becomes the solid, reliable schedule.

To some degree, I am a scheduler. When I first set out to do my business full time, I suffered under those vague timetables. To make sure I got my day moving in the right direction, I had to recognize what times were the most productive for certain tasks and then arrange my day around that.

There is another benefit with a schedule. I can do any unpleasant task and throw my heart into it so long as I know when it will end. If I know that I must make 10 cold calls today, I commit to doing it from 1:30 – 2:30 pm. With that motivation, I often will make more than the required amount because I am on the clock.

A job seeker's morning schedule might look something like this:
7:00 am – feed pets on Facebook
7:15 am – read Google alerts
8:00 am – review employment websites
10:00 am – work on LinkedIn network
11:30 am – lunch

Yes, those are my "Happy Pets" from Facebook. It may sound silly, but you need to build in time for "recess" and lunch. Those breaks are just as important as the work. Additionally, some tasks could easily consume your day but may not be very productive, such as constantly checking your email. By limiting the amount of time for those pits, you become more effective.

Schedules can also be used to block out time to accomplish difficult tasks. I know that I frequently need to mark large blocks of time in my calendar to make sure I can get my writing work done. Without a specific time to do it, I will quickly fall behind.

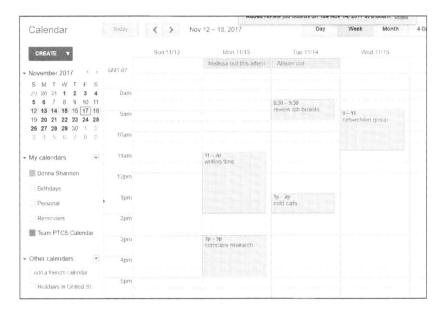

There are some traps with relying on a schedule. You don't want to get thrown off-balance just because something unexpected happens, like a cancelled appointment. The other problem is not building enough structure. You need a certain level of personal accountability, otherwise Happy Pets may become more important than those horrible cold calls.

Deadlines:

Do you work best when there is a looming deadline? Does a ticking clock motivate you? Then setting some real deadlines for your job search can increase your overall effectiveness. Some of these deadlines could be knowing that unemployment requires five contacts made by Friday or seeing that a job will be closing on June 30th.

Many deadline-driven people have challenges with the job search. After all, there are few "real" heavy deadlines, except for outside forces like the governmental requirements to keep your unemployment. Most companies won't even give you a closing date on their job postings. As a result, some deadliners will procrastinate just to generate that sense of urgency necessary to do their best work.

Overall, you need to acquire some tools and best practices to create real deadlines for your work. For example, most job postings will get the majority of their candidates in the first week of the job posting. Even if there is no official closing date, it is a safe bet that HR will start screening candidates 5 business days after the posting opens. Use this guideline to make sure you get your resume in to the job before this unspoken deadline.

Building accountability tools creates deadlines as well. This is one of the main functions of a career coach. Knowing that you need to complete your homework before your next appointment can be a great motivator, as well as adding in the accountability factor. If you can't afford a coach for the entire length of your job search, seek out a job search buddy.

 A job search buddy is someone you meet with on a regular basis to compare how well your job searches are going. However, don't let it slip into being just social coffee once a week. You need to set clear goals for each other and target results to make sure that both of you keep moving forward.

Lists:

Lists are my personal favorite. I find it extremely cathartic to create a list of my tasks for the week and, as I finish each one, physically pick up a pen and cross that item off the list. It doesn't have to be anything fancy. I literally use a sticky note and a pen. Throughout the week, I refer to the list to give me focus and help me stay on track.

On the surface, list makers almost look like goal makers. After all, the process of creating the SMART goals is the same. However, it is the reward that is different. A goal-driven person gains the sense of accomplishment by meeting and exceeding the goals, while a list maker gets a thrill from crossing things out.

Some sample weekly list items include:

- Work on LinkedIn profile

- Check out networking groups

- Look up three target companies

List makers do have traps as well. I know some people who devote way too much time into developing the list itself. A weekly "to-do" list should be action-oriented short phrases, not a novel with details under each little thing. Some list makers suffer from the opposite problem, where they can't get beyond the big picture to develop the smaller action items for their job search.

Consider all the steps for your job search. In this book, we give you many resources to spark your brain on what those items should be. Certainly, the job seeker's job description is a good place to start, especially when trying to break the chains of just looking at the job boards repeatedly.

Applying Your Work Style

When arranging your job search, always be playing to your strengths. While everyone should be developing SMART tools, how you execute them may be different. Do you need the challenging goals to pump up your blood? Do you need a specific schedule and set routine? How can you create deadlines that are meaningful? Or will your list bring focus to what you need to get done this week?

My Favorite Workstyle and How I Will Apply It:

Creating Structure for Your Job Search

As a manager, you need to make sure your job search employee is set up for success. Part of this means establishing structure, especially in the areas of time, tools, location, personal discipline, and buy-in from loved ones.

Recognize that the job search will take some time. Whether you are a schedule-driven person or not, if you are serious about your job search, set aside some time every day or during the week to work on it. This may mean backing off on your favorite pastimes, but the long-term goal outweighs the short-term pleasures.

Make sure you have effective tools for your job search. In modern terms, having high-speed internet and reliable access to a computer are vital. Fortunately, many websites like LinkedIn offer extremely reliable and robust mobile apps for your job search. However, trying to do an entire job search from an iPad is not only less than ideal, it can also create complications. For example, if an employer wants you to complete some documentation in Word and you only have Apple's Pages word processing software, your value as a candidate decreases severely. Although using the free online versions of Word, Pages, and even Google Docs are possible solutions, they can only provide simple formatting which will often look different from one computer to another – an annoying glitch that I refer to as "Word creep." By the way, the full computer versions of Word and Office tend to minimize this effect, but nothing is guaranteed!

Finally, you need to have buy-in from your family, loved ones, and friends. Job seeking takes time, and sometimes that means taking time away from them. If that is not an option, you will need to make other sacrifices, such as staying up late or waking up early to work on your job search. Remember, this is temporary. But if you don't invest the time, attention, and space, that temporary job search is going to stretch out longer and longer. Just remember what you agreed to when you identified what you are willing and not willing to do to conduct a successful job search.

Now that you are clear about how to manage yourself, let's put into play that next essential management tool: a proven business strategy to systemize and improve your actual job search.

Chapter 4: The Sales Process

YOUR JOB SEARCH IS A SALES PROCESS. Like it or not, you are now a salesman in addition to being a manager. Of course, the product you are selling is yourself. As such, you need to implement a sales process or pipeline to organize your opportunities and focus on the ones that look most promising.

There are six stages to the Job Search Sales Process: Prospecting, Qualifying, Discovery, Proposals, Interview, and Job Offer:

1. Prospecting = Lead Generation
2. Qualifying = Removing Undesirable Jobs
3. Discovery = Research
4. Proposal = Submitting the Resume and Cover Letter
5. Interview = Interview Prospective Employers/ More Qualifying
6. Job Offer = Negotiation

Prospecting

Goal: Generate as Many Leads as Possible

Prospecting is the pure hunting and gathering aspect of the job search. If we were looking for an Executive Assistant job, we could think of prospecting as "all Executive Assistant jobs in the Denver metro area."

Prospecting includes searching the job boards, networking strategies, tracking target companies, and following the news.

Basically, any source that generates a lead is prospecting, whether it is a formally posted job or one that is lurking in the hidden job market.

Qualifying

Goal: Screen Out the Undesirables

Good news, everybody! This is NOT about the employers screening you out. This is YOU getting to pass judgement on the employers.

Consider all the criteria you laid out with your 4 L's exercise, the Love it, Like It, Live with It, and Loathe It aspects of your work. Use these factors to take the leads and throw out the ones that don't align with your passions or just have too many of the things that you hate. Next, consider other factors that lead to your job satisfaction. Too far away? Gone. Bad company culture? Lose it. Not enough pay or opportunity for advancement? Sayonara. Once you get rid of the unwanted jobs, you can concentrate on researching the top choices.

Note: Don't Mix Prospecting and Qualifying

Have you ever found a job online that got you really excited? You quickly read the company's website and immediately started filling out the job application, but after 30 or 45 minutes into this horrible form, you weren't even sure if you wanted the job or not? If so, you just trapped yourself.

Prospecting and Qualifying hit the brain in different ways. Prospecting is all about hunting, while Qualifying is analysis. It is more effective to separate them into two different steps. For example, you may devote an hour to prospecting jobs on LinkedIn, either saving the possible positions or emailing them to yourself. Later that same day, go read those opportunities again. How well do they stack up to your established criteria? If the surface looks like a viable prospect, move them down the funnel and into...

Discovery

Goal: Research the Company as Much as Possible, Including Tracking Down Key Managers

Now that we have some possible jobs or target companies, we want to dive into a heavy-duty research phase. Basically, we want to find out as much as we can about the company, including the key managers and their contact information. In particular, you need to know:

- Their corporate mission

- Their products and services

- Their performance in the marketplace

- Their competition

- Their challenges

- Key managers, especially within your target department as well as all senior leaders and decision makers

- Don't overly focus on the names of their in-house recruiters or HR department

Don't waste your time tracking down the names of their in-house recruiters or HR department. In fact, most HR professionals don't want to be contacted by job seekers. That's why they state, "no phone calls" in the job postings. Now, if you happen to run into the recruiter's name during your research, don't shy away from using it in the greeting of your cover letter. Similarly, if the recruiter left their name and profile visible on the LinkedIn job posting, you can send a quick note or message to let him or her know that you applied for the job. Other than that, most contacts made to the HR department are like talking to a wall – especially in large companies. However, there are no rules against contacting hiring managers directly. Remember, they are often just as frustrated with HR as you.

When researching a company, the first layer of information can be found directly on the company website. However, to be an outstanding candidate, you need to reach beyond the obvious sources. In fact, Discovery is one of the more intensive portions of your job search. This makes a definitive difference in identifying ways to fill the company's needs – which leads to more interviews.

* See Appendix I, Sources For Industry And Company Research

The First Three Stages: Vital or Time Wasters?

Notice that the first three stages in the sales funnel – Prospecting, Qualifying, and Discovery – are the largest. This is because most of your time will be spent doing these types of activities. Unfortunately, they can also feel the least rewarding. Nobody really enjoys spending hours poring over the job boards or trying to make connections with strangers on LinkedIn. Who would get a thrill from researching a company for two hours, just to discover that they are moving their operations out-of-state in a month?

Do not lose hope. While these steps can feel frustrating, they are vital for your job search. Consider this: a successful salesman will make a sale 10-20% of the time. However, that figure relates to the amount of proposals that are submitted. She may have gone through 100 leads to get to the 10 viable prospects. For a job seeker, that translates into getting a single phone interview out of every 10 applications sent. You may have to look at 50-100 job postings to get to the ones that meet your criteria and goals. The trick is to make the first three stages as streamlined and systematic as possible so that when you do send your resume, it will be targeted and effective.

Proposal

Goal: Create a Targeted, Relevant Resume and Cover Letter

Once you have a good idea about the company, the position, and the key managers, it is time to modify your resume and cover letter to fit this specific situation. While I don't endorse completely rewriting your resume to each and every job, tweaking the keywords and achievements to fit the job description can be effective in moving your application through the HR screening process.

Whether you change your resume or not, you absolutely want to customize your cover letter for each job. In fact, you may use a different cover letter for the HR department and the hiring manager, as their understanding of what is vital for the job may be different.

When reaching out to a company that may not have any posted job openings, the proposal stage is critical. You need to convince the manager that you can help with one of three things: that you can make money, save money, or solve problems. If you can prove that while being entirely relevant for their needs, your phone will start to ring.

The Job Interview

Goal: Interview the Company While Putting Your Best Foot Forward

Interviewing is a two-way street. While most job seekers sweat about their own performance, you need to be aware of the surroundings and ask tough questions to make sure the job meets your criteria.

When preparing for the interview, remember to review your research. However, always be aware of the tone and emphasis that the company portrays in the interview. After all, the reality of the job, the culture, and the opportunities may be very different than what they put forth in their public face – both good and bad.

Job Offer

Goal: Negotiate

No matter what the job offer is, you can always negotiate for a better deal. Believe it or not, most HR departments already have a second offer in their back pocket.

However, most job seekers don't try to negotiate or counteroffer. According to a 2016 survey by Glassdoor.com, 59% of US workers accepted the first salary they were offered. (https://www.glassdoor.com/blog/3-5-u-s-employees-negotiate-salary/) In fact, this statistic is more intimidating when looking at gender: 68% of women accepted the first offer, compared to only 52% of men who did not negotiate. This is often cited as one of the many reasons for the gender wage gap. You won't get a better salary if you don't ask for it.

While this may seem like an issue when being hired, it sets up the new employee for depressed salaries throughout their tenure. After all, raises are usually based on a percentage of the current salary. If you come in too low when first hired, the disparity can follow you throughout your employment at the company.

Negotiations include more than just the money. Sometimes that can't be negotiated. Think about the other factors that were important in your overall goals. Would the company be willing to do some work-from-home or flexible schedules? Is it possible to negotiate additional paid time off? Are there other side perks, such as a company phone or laptop that you can use after hours? How about either more travel or capping the amount of time on the road?

Remember your overall goals – this is your roadmap to negotiating a situation that fits your needs the best.

Chapter 5: The Job Search Plan

NOW THAT WE UNDERSTAND THE SALES PROCESS, let's convert those concepts into the specific, actionable steps of the job search plan itself.

The 9 Step Job Search Plan

1. Get your tools in order
2. Efficiently search for jobs online
3. Create prospecting lists
4. Research employers
5. Conduct structured networking
6. Submit targeted resumes
7. Prepare for and ace interviews
8. Track your activity and follow up regularly
9. Evaluate your progress

At first glance, these steps may sound daunting. Do not be discouraged – each step is designed to teach you solid skills that will lead to the next step. Plus, everything within the Job Search Plan does relate back to the sales process.

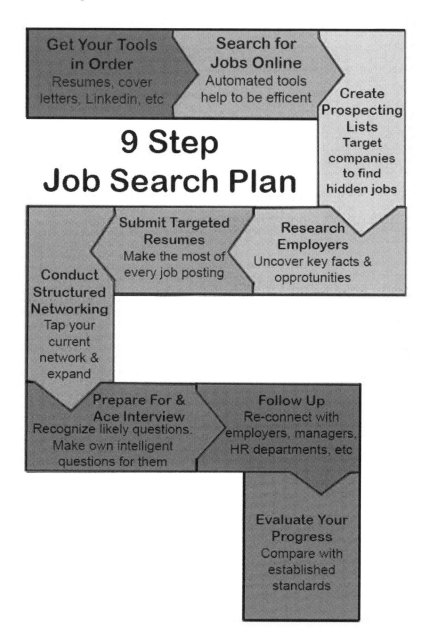

Step 1: Get your tools in order

First and foremost, you need to have your job search tools ready to go. This includes your resume, LinkedIn profile, cover letter templates, thank you letter templates, and networking cover letter templates completed before you start doing outreach. [For more information on resume writing, please review "How to Get a Job Without Going Crazy" (2nd Edition) by Donna Shannon.]

Now, let's talk about your social media. And I don't mean LinkedIn. If you are on any other social media platform – Facebook, Twitter, Instagram, whatever – just make sure everything on there is PG-rated. You don't need to start a new account if you don't have one, but if you are participating in these communities, just make sure that there is nothing that would give a future employer pause. Keep your nose clean!

Step 2: Efficiently search for jobs online [Prospecting]

Chances are, you have heard the dismal statistics: only 10–20% of job seekers find their next job on the job boards. It is true that this is a hard fight to win. However, those depressing numbers don't consider the other half of the job search: getting in touch with the hiring manager as well as following HR's instructions for applying to the job.

In your job search, you don't want to leave any stone unturned. While using employment sites like Indeed, ZipRecruiter, and even LinkedIn may not be the most lucrative area for job seeking, we don't want to completely ignore them.

The big tip with the job boards is to use them effectively and efficiently. They are excellent LEAD sources, not the be-all, end-all for getting the job. In other words, it falls into the *Prospecting* category for your job search. In Chapter 6: Searching for Jobs Online we will discuss ways to make these searches as streamlined and automated as possible, so you don't miss out on a highly qualified job lead.

Step 3: Create prospecting lists for target companies, industries, and networking opportunities [Prospecting]

Before applying to any of the jobs listed on the employment websites, create and add them to your Prospecting list. Additionally, this list will also include any potential opportunities in the hidden job market. This is done by identifying desirable employers – whether they have a job opening or not – and creating a systematic plan for researching them.

Prospecting lists are also used to track your research on identifying hidden jobs. A hidden job is any position that isn't openly advertised. To find these, you need to be in tune with what is going on in your community and your industry. Discovering influential companies or those experiencing growth is a great way to anticipate their needs, which is the big secret in landing a job at your target employers.

In Chapter 7: Essential Organization and Research Tools, I will give you very specific strategies to easily stay on top of your research and uncover different sources. Additionally, Appendix I: Research Resources provides excellent starting points and specific websites.

Step 4: Research employers [Qualifying and Discovery]

Once your company prospecting list is in place, it's time to start researching them and move on to the _Discovery_ phase. The goal is to research 5 to 10 different companies every week. If you are trying to break into a large corporation or organization, focus on conducting thorough research on fewer targets, such as concentrating on multiple departments within one company.

So, what exactly are you trying to find out? Basically, everything that you can – especially the pieces that relate to your overall job goals. Obviously, you want to start by reaching their website and determining the basics, such as their mission, products, services, and leaders. Check out the careers page not only for open jobs but also insight into their process or hiring trends.

The most important piece of research for either a posted or hidden job is to track down that hiring manager and get your resume directly into his or her hands. Finding these decision makers is probably the most important part of the Discovery process. All these strategies are cover in depth in Chapter 8: Track Down the Hiring Manager.

Step 5: Conduct structured networking [Prospecting, Qualifying, and Discovery]

Ever hear the rumor that 80% of jobs are won by networking? Sounds intimidating, especially if you aren't an active networker, a natural introvert, or if you get intimidated by reaching out to strangers. In some ways, this number is inflated. In fact, networking includes everything from attending industry-related events to your Aunt Martha forwarding you a job that she saw posted on Indeed.

Networking is so essential that it actually covers three parts of the sales process: *Prospecting*, *Qualifying*, and *Discovery*. Yet, for the average job seeker, this is the most intimidating part of the job search. No wonder most people are willing to rework their resume for the millionth time rather than go to an after-hours networking event! Fortunately, networking is more than just shaking hands with strangers.

The idea of implementing a structured networking plan is designed to:
- Relieve networking anxiety.

- Make the most of your current network.

- Develop methods for increasing your network with strategies that you will actually use.

- Address multiple networking platforms, from events to social media.

- Continue to build on your success.

We will dive into these specific strategies in Chapter 9: Structured Networking.

Step 6: Submit targeted resumes and applications [Proposal]

Once you know more about the company, it is time to make sure your resume has the best chance of maneuvering the applicant tracking system, or ATS. While the main goal is to get in touch with hiring managers directly, the cold fact is sometimes that is not possible. For example, some companies are very regimented in their hiring practices, which means that even when the hiring manager receives a resume, they are forced by policy to send it back to HR. In case of government jobs, this is even more restrictive as hiring managers are legally bound to only consider candidates who have successfully navigated the HR screening processes.

 In general, I am not a fan of customizing resumes for every single job. However, when faced with a stringent screening process used by large corporations, government jobs, and regulated industries, taking the time to customize the resume to fit the specific position becomes a more worthwhile activity. In Chapter 10: Tweaking Your Resume, I will show you how to quickly and accurately customize your resume for different jobs. **Tweaking your resume should only take 30 to 45 minutes;** if you spend longer than that, you needed a better base resume in the first place. Sometimes that means having different base resumes for the overall target jobs, such as one for sales and one for marketing – while similar, they do require different keywords.

 **NOTE:** regardless of whether you change your resume or not, you *always* want to tweak your cover letter to match the specific position. This way, you can show the company and the managers that you understand their needs. Even better, try to show them how you can do one of three things: make money, save money, or solve problems. If you can hit them with a pitch like this, they will certainly take notice.

Step 7: Prepare for and ace job interviews [More Qualifying]

Interviewing is both a goal and a step-in job searching. You want your resume and networking efforts to lead to solid interviews; and, once there, you want to be able to present yourself well. Keep in mind that, during the interview itself, you are still qualifying the employers, finding out if the job is a good fit for you while setting up a position of strength for the final negotiations.

Preparing for an interview takes a lot more effort than just reading the company's website or reviewing the managers' LinkedIn profiles. Because this is such a critical step for your job search, we will dive deeply into this during Chapter 11: Interviewing Practices To Know Before You Go and Chapter 12: Strategies To Ace The Interview.

Step 8: Track your activity and follow up with employers, managers, and contacts

Do you know the difference between a good salesman and a great one? Follow-up skills. From tracking everything they do to implementing effective follow-up strategies, they know where every possible lead stand in the sales pipeline and are making efforts to move the best prospects forward.

Notice that the first part of following up is keeping track of your activities. Basically, if you don't write something down, it did not happen. You need to make note of everything that you do for your search, including dating every entry. For example, your Prospecting List already indicates areas to enter notes and key dates. This way, when you reach out to the company again, you know what the last action taken was.

Following up can be intimidating for many people. Don't worry. Just remember that every piece of follow up that you do, from sending quality thank-you notes after the job interview or just reaching out to someone on LinkedIn following a networking event, adds to your likelihood of landing a great job. Just remember to track everything – if you don't write it down, it didn't happen!

Step 9: Evaluate your progress

On a monthly basis, you want to evaluate your progress and make sure that you are moving in the right direction. This includes reviewing your resume and LinkedIn profile to make sure they are still conveying in the right message. Similarly, look at your job search agents on the employment websites and make certain they are sending the right types of positions, based on your goals and target jobs. Look at your networking efforts and identify any areas of strength or weakness.

Following is a table to evaluate your job search. For each line, write down the activity itself, such as looking up jobs on Indeed or attending a networking group. Additionally, take into consideration what part of the sales process does this activity address. Everything should relate in some way to the pipeline itself. Finally, write down what IS working and what is NOT working.

Activity	Point of the Sales Process	What is Working	What is NOT Working
Attending the Brown Bag Job Search Group	Prospecting Qualifying	Made valuable contacts Learned job searching techniques Learned about hiring procsess at Channel 6 Is free	Not many job leads
Indeed.com	Prospecting	Finding new opprotunities Tracking target companies Largest employ-ment website for jobs available	Possible scams Lots of competition

While looking at your activities for the month, look at not only the quantifiable metrics but also the overall value of each. Sometimes, an activity may not lead to jobs, but they remain valuable in their own right because they contribute to your professional development, boost morale, or just help with getting out of the house on a regular basis. On this sample, the Brown Bag Job Search Group is a networking group that I have run for job seekers for many years. Every month, this free meeting offers open networking time as a well as a presentation related to some aspect of job searching. As a result, some of the things that are working for job seekers are the learning opportunities and chances to connect with other job seekers. Similarly, since I used to work in HR at one of the local TV stations, a job seeker can learn more about those processes. Unfortunately, not a lot of job leads are generated. Given this evaluation, a job seeker can now make an informed decision on whether to continue with the group or not – do the benefits outweigh the time taken to attend? For many people, the answer is yes.

So, What are You Doing All Day?

Now that you have an overall plan, what is the best way to implement it? In addition to the Job Search Plan Checklist, let's break down the types of activities you should be doing on a daily, weekly, and monthly basis.

Daily tasks:

- Email.
- Social media.
- Company, industry, or networking research.
- Tracking progress.

Every day, you need to try to check your email. Sounds obvious, right? The real trick is to focus on the emails that support your job search, rather than taking an hour a day to dive into your personal interests. This is one of the reasons why people often make an email address just for their job search.

Second, get involved with your social media, preferably LinkedIn. This does not mean that you need to spend hours within the site. Instead, find ways to streamline this process and still get involved. For example, one of the best ways to build your reputation in LinkedIn is to get involved in multiple Groups. Every day, your Groups will send you a summary digest of the discussions. When you see one that interests you, click on the link and make a comment. You just made a positive impact on your social media, and – best of all – it only took a moment to do it. [For more information on managing your LinkedIn efforts, visit Donna Shannon's online course, "Using LinkedIn to Get a Job Without Going Crazy." https://goo.gl/vCPsfG]

Third, a part of every day needs to be devoted to your research and discovery efforts. Whether this is looking up companies on your prospecting list or hunting for hiring managers for a posted job, this is the real heart of your job search.

Finally, track your progress. When you get in the habit of making notes every time you accomplish a task – no matter how small – this will build a valuable database for future use. Not only that, you can see your little successes that will lead to the big goals.

Weekly Tasks:

- Checking job boards.
- Apply to appropriate jobs.
- Pick the research targets.
- Get OUT of the house.
- Follow up on previous contacts/applications.

Technically, you need to be checking your job boards every day. However, you need to rotate them, so you are looking at a different website or job search agent every single day. This means that you will be looking at any given job board on a weekly basis. This is fully explained in Chapter 6: Searching for Jobs Online.

Don't forget to set up job search alerts from your top target employer's company websites. Not everybody pays the money for a job ad, either because they don't need to advertise, or their industry is more hidden. For example, some time ago I wanted to work at Regis University in Denver. However, they don't advertise their jobs. So, I had to go onto their Careers page on a weekly basis and search for new jobs manually.

Second, apply to jobs. Even if you don't find your dream job posted within a week, you need to apply to at least three jobs to create your quantifiable metrics.

Third, pick out your new research targets from your prospecting list. In any given week, you want to research 5–10 companies, consisting of both targets for the hidden job market and employers who are advertising their positions.

Fourth, get out of your house. Go to a networking event. Go help a friend. Go to a fun activity or new social group you found on Meetup.com. Whatever it is, build in a change of scenery and attitude. This is critical for your motivation and maintaining a positive attitude.

Finally, remember to follow up on past contacts or opportunities. When recording and tracking your progress, always build in a follow-up date. This way, you aren't overly hounding these valuable contacts, but you aren't letting them languish too long either.

Monthly Tasks:

- Job search assessment.

- Review your tools: LinkedIn, website settings, resumes, and letters.

- Tap your network on the shoulder.

Every month be sure to conduct a Job Search Assessment to make sure that all your activities are producing results. The essence of a successful job search is putting more effort into the strategies that are working while reducing those that are sucking up your time and attention without providing a benefit.

Second, look at all your materials and tools. Are you still sending the right message? If you have been doing a lot of customizations, are you still retaining the voice of your original resume and cover letters? Is it becoming quicker and more efficient to tweak the resume for different jobs? Are the job search agents producing the right types of jobs?

Finally, take a moment to tap your network on the shoulder and just remind them that you are still looking for a position, especially the people closest to you professionally and personally. Many times, people want to help, but they just get caught up in their own lives and forget about your situation. When reaching out, always ask the other person what you can do for them. Networks work both ways, and if you aren't adding value to the people in your life, they will be less likely to share valuable contacts with you.

Chapter 6: Searching for Jobs Online

MOST PEOPLE START THEIR JOB SEARCH by looking at the online job boards or websites, including Indeed.com, LinkedIn, ZipRecruiter, CareerBuilder, and even Glassdoor.com. And then they wait. As we already explored, this by itself is not necessarily the best way to find a job, but these sites can be a good source for lead generation. For that reason, you don't want to ignore them, but we do need to streamline them so they don't become the main source of the job search.

Safety Tips for Your Job Search

One of my Denver clients recently called me with an unfortunate but common problem:

"I just got called by the police – they discovered an identity theft ring which had stolen my information from an online job application," he said, totally despondent and heartbroken. "I guess I'm lucky because the cops caught them, but I still have to deal with cleaning up the mess they made..."

In recent years, identity theft and other scams that target job seekers has seen a sharp increase. It is estimated that 50% of job ads on craigslist.com are fraudulent. Compared to a rate of approximately 30% in 2008, it is easy to see that the thieves are banking on the desperation of job seekers. In fact, any of the sites that are relatively inexpensive to post jobs or ones that can hit multiple sites from one source – notably Indeed.com and ZipRecruiter – are very attractive to scam artists.

Fortunately, you can easily protect yourself from such scams.

Too good to be true? Probably...

One time, my husband, Ryan, found a job on Indeed that looked tailor-made for him, with a posted starting salary that was about $20,000 more than the average local pay for the job. Excited but skeptical, he asked me to check it out before he applied. My first step was to go directly to the employer's website. Even though the job posting on Indeed had the company's logo and the exact same language as the original job on the employer's website, it was painfully clear that the company was only operating in Tennessee, with no plans to open a branch in Colorado.

The entire listing was a spoofed job, set up by scammers to capture job seeker's identities.

See why research is so important? It will save you from being a victim of identity theft. Keep a look-out for these other common strategies that scammers use.

Protect your information

One of the common tricks is to direct job seekers to an online application. While many legitimate companies use online applications, or Applicant Tracking Systems (ATS), look out for ones that require too much personal information.

If the application asks for any of this information, do NOT fill it in:
- Social Security number.
- Birthdate (a legal application should only ask if you are over 18).

- Bank account information (often disguised as trying to set up your direct deposit).

- Mother's maiden name (often needed to establish false credit under your name).

- Previous names used (it may be prefaced with the company stating that they need to conduct a background check. A legitimate HR department may ask for this after the interview, but very rarely do they invest in the expense of a background check without actually speaking to the candidate first.)

If you are still interested in the job after running into these requests, call the company directly. Of course, look up that information yourself rather than calling the number on the suspicious website. If the company's name is not listed on the website, definitely run the other way.

Exception to the rule: Government jobs

Government positions, and especially US federal jobs, have their own quirks for candidates. Basically, you are required to tell them anything and everything you've ever done. This specifically includes not just your social security number, but such uncomfortable details as your complete salary history. Don't worry; you are safe on these sites. Please note that this book does not cover in detail the specific tactics for landing a federal government job. It requires a different etiquette, tactics, and time frame. If you want to work for the government, look at the requirements for application on their website first: www.usajobs.gov. If you are intrigued with the possibilities, invest in some books or classes that specifically address federal positions before you apply. However, state, county, and city jobs are often run like a large corporation in their screening procedures.

Don't accept packages

An older scam that still hasn't completely gone away is the offer to help someone run their purchasing business. While it used to show up as a job posting on low-level job sites like Craigslist.com, now people are sending an "offer" to individuals as LinkedIn messages. Usually coming from someone across the country or who "travels a lot," the job sounds like a great way to make part-time money. All you have to do is receive the packages and ship them forward.

The first few deals may work out. However, then as you "prove yourself" on the job, you get asked to make purchases on the employer's behalf, with a promise to pay you back plus interest. Here, the scam can run two ways: either you never get reimbursed or else the employer asks for your banking information to send you money.

Anytime someone asks for banking info is a bad sign.

Legitimate professional shoppers and art dealers do not operate this way. They already have a network that they use for these services.

Want to be a "secret shopper?"

Here's another oldie that has evolved onto LinkedIn. Like the packages scam, you get a message from someone that you just connected to on LinkedIn. Of course, they are always the one who asked to connect with you. Immediately after the connection is made, you get a long message describing all the "wonderful" benefits of being a secret shopper and how they have made "thousands of dollars every month – for just a few hours of work!" Yeah, sorry, that's not real. Just disconnect from this person as soon as you can and report them to LinkedIn.

A variation of this is when the scammers hack your legitimate friends' LinkedIn accounts. If one of your long-standing contacts sends you a message like this, email them back (off LinkedIn) and make sure they are aware. Then they can take the steps to reclaim their account before LinkedIn shuts it down completely.

Work-at-home (WAH)

In the modern world, legitimate work-at-home (WAH) or remote positions have skyrocketed. It's a great solution for both employees and employers. However, that means that it's also attractive to scammers.

Traditional WAH Scams

In previous years, it was a lot easier to identify the scams from these common traits:

- You must pay for training.

- You buy materials to assemble items for resale (either you can't sell the items, or the "employer" won't pay you for the work performed).

- Bogus direct deposit forms.

Modern WAH opportunities and the Side Hustle

While many of these may not be full-blown scams, they can be a difficult way to make a living. For example, many employers make their remote employees independent contractors so that they don't have to pay benefits nor worry about complying with different employment laws from state-to-state – not to mention saving money on payroll processing, workers' comp, and the employer's portion of payroll taxes.

If you are serious about a work-from-home opportunity, check out **www.Flexjobs.com.** While you do have to pay to see the full jobs listings, FlexJobs researches each and every job posted to make sure it is a legitimate offering from a real company. This includes part-time, full-time, and contract positions.

Many people take jobs within the "gig economy" to carry them through, such as ride-sharing companies like Uber and Lyft. As more and more companies get creative with this source of talent, it is spreading into multiple different industries, including hospitality, trades, and services like pet sitting. Depending on how diligent you are with committing to a regular work schedule, you can earn a full-time living with these gigs. Frequently, these opportunities are called the "side hustle" to make extra money on your own terms and without committing to a set work schedule.

Questions to Ask

Whenever you are considering these options, be sure to ask YOUR-SELF these questions:

- Am I self-motivated enough to completely manage my own time?

- Am I willing to take on the expense of providing and maintaining my own equipment, such as my laptop or car? Even though these are tax-deductible, you will need to pay out of your own pocket initially.

- Do I have proper work space within my home to take a remote position?

- Do I work better in a team environment?

- Do I focus better at home or does a specific work location help me concentrate?

When screening potential opportunities, be sure to ask the **EM-PLOYER** these questions:

- How many hours do your most successful employees work to reach a target salary of $XX?

- What traits do your most successful contractors share?

- For gigs like Uber or Lyft, when is the most lucrative time of day to login to the app? How about the most lucrative area of town? (After all, if you aren't available to work 2 am on Friday night, you miss top dollars!)

- If this is a sales position, how is commission calculated and how do I earn the top bonuses?

- If this is a regular employment role, is there any reimbursement for technology expenses, such as cell phone allowance or internet?

- What type of technology does the company provide, if any?

Many economists see the gig economy as a solution for low unemployment in key industries. It gives both employers and workers flexibility, especially for Millennials and Generation Z, who show more favoritism towards a work/life blend that allows them to manage their own time 100%. In the gig economy, you can choose when you work, when you play, and when you live your life. In the future, we may see even more traditional companies began offering the remote work options a few days a week to not only save on office space overhead but to also cater to this evolving notion of a "normal work schedule."

Where Are the Jobs?

In Appendix I: Research Resources, I offer a lot of different websites to check out for potential job openings. You want to use a good mix of sources, from the large sites like LinkedIn to the specialty sites for your specific industry. Even some of the original pioneers like Career-Builder.com and Monster.com can be helpful, especially if you are open to working with recruiters or temporary agencies. Specialty sites like Dice.com for IT professionals and EngineerJobs.com for engineers address just one sector. A quick Google search of your target title plus "jobs" will quickly reveal the top sites. A similar search on industries will reveal more sites, especially ones run by associations, such as https://www.coloradononprofits.org/careers, which hosts nonprofit jobs in Colorado or https://www.jobs.shrm.org, which is the national association website for the Society of Human Resources.

Once you have identified your top job sites, establish your accounts and start setting up your job search agents or job search alerts. These are preset searches that can feed you new results on a daily or weekly basis. These automated emails will help populate your *Prospecting* list.

By the way, practice Boolean search terms to help you narrow down the results. Not sure what those are? It's how we used to quantify our search results before Google got too smart for our own good. Check out this article by Glen Cathey to see how they work. "Basic Boolean Search Operators and Query Modifiers Explained:" http://booleanblackbelt.com/2008/12/basic-boolean-search-operators-and-query-modifiers-explained/.

Depending on the site, they may call your saved search terms the job search agent, job search alert, or simply the saved search. For example, on Indeed, look for any prompt that says something like, "Be the first to see new program manager jobs in Denver, CO" after your search, followed by a field for your email address. That is your job search alert. By the way, you can always edit or even cancel these alerts on any job board by going to your account and looking for the "Job Alerts" listing. (By the way, LinkedIn is a little different. Your alerts are under the "Jobs" tab, right underneath the Search fields for the jobs themselves.)

 While you're setting up your job search agents, remember to make each site send you relevant jobs on a different day. As I mentioned in Chapter 5, you only want to look at each website once a week, although you will be looking at a site every day. You are just rotating them; for example, you might look at Indeed on Monday, LinkedIn on Tuesday, ZipRecruiter on Wednesday, Dice.com on Thursday, and CareerBuilder on Friday. Similarly, you can rotate the search terms for each day:

So, why do you want to do this?

Have you ever been frustrated by seeing nothing but the same jobs, over and over, because you are literally looking at the same job board every single day?

That's a bad habit that you need to stop immediately.

In fact, not only is this unproductive, it creates a false sense of scarcity. If you look at the same website every single day for weeks, you see a lot of jobs being repeated. In fact, you may only see one or two new jobs appear each day – if even that much. It doesn't take long for your brain to get frustrated and proclaim, "Why am i doing this? There is nothing but the same jobs every single day!" This leads to frustration, and even depression, that can stop your job search in its tracks.

Mon	Tues	Wed	Thurs	Fri	Sat
Linkedin	Indeed	Zip Recruiter	The Ladders	Career Builder	
					Sun

Notes:

Follow Up!

When you rotate the job boards you view, you get to see fresh opportunities every day. Plus, most HR departments will accept applications for at least five business days, so your chances of missing out on an opportunity are minimized.

THIS is how you automate and streamline the prospecting on the major employment websites – AND save yourself from going crazy.

Thinning the herd of employment sites

Within a couple of weeks, you will notice which websites attract good opportunities and those which, well, just suck. The good news is that you can ALWAYS edit or delete your job search agents, meaning that you can drop those sites that don't produce quality jobs. This allows you to spend your time on the most successful ones, further streamlining your online job searching.

Posting Your Resume Online: Good idea or Bad idea?

Have you seen the ads giving statistic like "job seekers are more likely to find a job when they post their resume on such-n-such site?" That is true – but it does not mean that your resume must be visible to the entire world! Be conscious of the different posting options to control your online image.

Public

A public posting allows potential employers to view your resume, even when you did not apply for a job. Your resume and all your contact information will be visible in a search.

Confidential

A confidential posting is still public, but the website will hide your name and contact information, which might include the names and place of your current employer. Recruiters will be able to contact you by email through the employment website itself.

Private

No one can see your resume unless you apply for the job. It will not turn up in general searches. When you apply, the employer does get all your contact information.

Most people choose to post their resume privately – but it is still technically a posted resume, and that counts towards the job site's sales statistics. Websites use these statistics to sell their services to the employers.

Why would you post your resume publicly?

If you choose to post publicly, aggressive recruiters, 100% commission sales jobs or less-than-desirable employers might contact you. However, if you are in a high-demand, high-volume industry such as healthcare or if you are on a specialty site like Dice.com, it might be worth the risk.

When an employer searches through the resume database, it is called data mining. Employers pay money – and a lot of it – to conduct a search like this. In fact, it is often more expensive for the employer to conduct data mining than to pay for a simple job posting. That's why most employers do not use this feature to find employees. Typically, data mining is used to fill high-turnover positions, such as 100% commission sales jobs. Or worse: it could be a the thinly veiled selling opportunities, such as a "chance" to be your own boss selling insurance – but first you must pay for your classes, your license, their motivational books, and so on... you get the idea.

If you are not in a high-volume field, post your resume privately. Maintaining control on your online information is an important part of your job search.

A word of caution

If you are considering posting your resume on a 100% public website, such as Craigslist, think about it very carefully. This opens you to serious risks that go far beyond your job search. It makes your information accessible to scam artists, spammers, and any number of unsavory creatures. Reputable employers rarely look at these amateur resume postings. It is recommended that you only post your resume on websites that allow you control over who can and cannot view your information. If you still want to consider posting your resume online in such a forum, read their Personal Safety Tips before you do.

By the way, don't be scared to try websites like Craigslist – just DON'T post your resume on it. You can still apply to those jobs, so long as you do some due diligence to verify the validity of the opportunity first.

Special offers and upgrades on resume posting

Throughout the process of posting your resume, you will get a lot of advertising. Don't get cynical – this is how websites pay for their free services to you. That doesn't mean you have to buy anything, including offers from the website itself. Think about what they are really offering; what sounds like a desirable service may not deliver the punch you're expecting. Here are a few examples:

Preferred Viewing or Resume Upgrade

A preferred viewing moves your resume to the top of the list during a recruiter's search. What they aren't telling you is that the preferred view applies to data mining. Remember the recruiters with the high-turnover jobs? If you pay for this service, you just became #1 on their list. Preferred viewing adds no value to the jobs you apply for directly, because they have no influence on an employer's independent ATS or databases. The ATS or the HR person will rate you based on your relevant qualifications, not your paid delivery service.

Resume Blasting

Resume blasting takes your pre-written resume and sends it out to a set list of recruiters or managers. How many depends on the level of service you buy. It seems like you can direct this to your target market because the service does ask for your keywords, careers, and locations. However, in practice, what they email is a stock cover letter (either yours or one they write for you) and one of your standard resumes. This turns your resume into spam!

Recruiters and managers recognize spam for what it is. If they bother to read it at all, it won't be effective. Why? Because it's a form letter. Employers only respond to cover letters that show your interest in their company. If you send an unsolicited resume, you must knock them dead with your knowledge, special skills, and experience. It is not possible to hit a pinpoint target by slinging "stuff" across the employment landscape and hoping something sticks. That is exactly what resume blasting does.

LinkedIn Premium Accounts

A big exception to the rule is LinkedIn. If you purchase a monthly LinkedIn account, this does have benefits beyond just visibility for your resume. True, they do give you a "preferred" status in the recruiter's queue when you apply for the job, but that is only one part of the package. Other helpful tools are improved searches, the ability to send people InMail messages if you aren't connected to them, and – most interestingly – statistics on who has already applied for any given job. In general, I recommend that job seekers use all of the free tips in my online course "Using LinkedIn to Get a Job Without Going Crazy" on Udemy.com first. Then, once you are fully proficient in LinkedIn, consider purchasing the Premium account for a few months. Just remember to cancel it when your job search is over.

Newsletters

Personally, I find newsletters helpful. They keep my mind focused on my job search, and they generally have good information. However, take all advice with a grain of salt. Some of the techniques can be old and aren't relevant anymore. There might be a gap between marketing theory and what real-world HR people and hiring managers use. Others can be trendy, focusing on techniques that not all employers will understand or use.

For example, some employment newsletters feature articles about unusual interview questions, providing insight into why they are used and how to answer them. In the real world, it is highly unlikely that you will be asked "how many quarters does it take to reach the height of the Empire State Building." These strange questions supposedly give insight into how you think, and making you sweat is an added bonus. In practice, most interviewers find this technique to be awkward – for them as well as the interviewee.

When reading these newsletters, weigh their advice against your own common sense. Does it sound far-fetched? Is it practical? Is it something that you would be comfortable doing in your own job search? Not all solutions work for all people.

Keep an open mind, but don't let your brain fall on the floor. Sign up for free newsletters from several different sources, such as TheMuse.com or Glassdoor, both of which provide articles for job seekers. Stay in touch with the employment game, but don't become discouraged if none of their suggestions seem reasonable to you. You can always cancel the free subscription later.

The Smart Way to Post Your Resume on Employment Websites

With all the major employment websites, you can choose between two options to post your resume online. You can either upload the Word document or PDF, or you can go through a step-by-step process to create your resume. In most cases, you want to upload the Word version; however, pay attention to some formatting quirks. (NOTE: I did not say Pages; Word is used by 90% of businesses, so convert your documents to Word or PDF if you are using an Apple device.)

Sometimes, you don't have a choice and you will be forced to use the online forms. This is often the case with online applications for a particular company. In that case, you do have to cut-and-paste various parts of your resume into their forms. If you created your Word resume in a modular format, each portion should stand on its own. Never try to type a brand-new resume in these forms; filling out forms creates bad writing. Even worse, you won't have spell-check or grammar indicators.

Always review any resume – whether you build it online or written in Word – before hitting the "submit" button. A few moments of review can make a difference between surviving the screening or turning into HR roadkill. Why? No matter how smart the ATS systems might be, they frequently misinterpret resume information, incorrectly parsing it into their forms. If you go back through it and correct these errors, you won't be screened out for a programming error on the ATS system's part.

How Your Resume Looks Online

Regardless of how you post your resume, there is a good chance that your formatting will be stripped, without warning and without your knowledge. A classic example of this conversion is Indeed.com: that ugly text-only document that you see is exactly what the employers are receiving.

Some internet sites are deceptive about this issue. When you navigate to the "employer view," it looks just like your Word document. However, that may or may not be what the employer will see. It all depends on how well their internal application system was integrated with the employment site.

Computers and AI Assumptions

Both commercial employment sites and individual employers will transfer your Word resume information into their own forms for their database or Applicant Tracking System (ATS). The forms are their backbone for the system. The system will catalogue and evaluate you, according to the information on your resume or in the stand-alone fields.

In any sizable company, these systems are indispensable for managing the flood of applications. As a job seeker, you will have to accept them as a necessary evil. Even when you've sent your resume to the hiring manager, you still need to apply through the company's online application. You don't want to be discredited because you didn't follow instructions outlined in the job posting. Since the system is critical to your job hunt, don't fall victim to bad assumptions on the computer's part.

The computer will assume your critical information based on common resume formats. This could be your job titles, company names, employment dates and education levels. While you can minimize some of the assumptions by keeping your critical information easily accessible, you still need to check the computer's work.

After you post your resume, take the time to review the summary pages or the applicant information fields. Verify that the information is correct. Look for missing pieces; sometimes, if the computer doesn't recognize a section, it overlooks it. This is particularly hazardous for references, summaries, and skill sets.

For your skill set, you may need to re-enter each and every skill along with proficiency levels and/or years of experience with it. It can be very time-consuming, but keep in mind that HR will use this information in screening and in making recommendations.

One issue with any online application or posted resume is that cover letters are an after-thought, as are references. Make sure to include yours because they can be a screening tool that some employers use to cut people. It is acceptable to paste a cover letter in the body of your resume to ensure it is included in the ATS. Add your references to the end of your Word resume as well.

A Note on education

Always list your degree, even if it is in an unrelated field. Education is a common screening tool, and the fact that you have a degree at all can make a difference. However, this does not mean that a lack of a degree will automatically screen you out. Many hiring managers don't care about the degree, so long as you can perform the work. Other careers demand a specific degree. How can you tell the difference?

Refer to back to the original job posting. Is a general degree mentioned, such as "BA/BS preferred," or do you need a specific one, such as "BA in Human Resources required?" The more detailed the request, the more important the degree is.

When you double-check the computerized entries, take note of how much information you can include in the fields. You may have a chance to pull out more information on the forms than what is listed on your resume. For example, the forms might allow you to enter your major and minor, or areas of special study. Unfortunately, the opposite may be true as well. Some of your resume's critical details could be sacrificed because the ATS lacks fields beyond the degree, year and school. If that's the case, you might need to re-emphasize this aspect of your background in your cover letter, especially if you are a new college graduate or if the degree is critical for your job.

Commercial employment websites like Monster emphasize degrees. This makes sense since many of their advertisers are colleges. They promote the importance of actual college experience. Don't be shaken if their advertising or marketing tactics make your feel less secure about your own education.

Look for ways to include non-formal education, such as online courses, independent study, workshops or classes that are listed as "professional development" on your resume. Computerized systems often fail to pull this information from a resume.

Dating yourself

You may be an older job seeker and you left your graduation date off your resume to mask the fact. Unfortunately, the system may force you to re-enter it. Some ATS require complete information or they won't let you continue to the next screen. It might also look strange to you if your work experience is limited to 15 years, but you graduated 25 years ago. It can be tempting to fill in the extra dates to show consistent employment.

If you choose to add any of this information, remember that most hiring managers won't see these details. What they care about is the fact that you have a degree, relevant experience, and the right skills. HR will give them the summary of the other information. To survive the screening, enter your complete information and reduce your risks.

Salary requirements

Some companies will require the Salary Requirements field on the application. Oh, what a killer, especially if you must state a single number rather than a range! You have two options: either use a ridiculous number like $1.00; or use the middle number from your real salary range, such as $70,000 if your range is $60,000 to $80,000 a year. If it is not a requirement, just leave it blank or use "negotiable."

Final Words on Electronic Job Searching

Online job searching is a critical part of your job search strategy. Take the time to make sure your resume is loaded correctly and that your profile fits with your targets. Be sure to hit the major employment sites, but don't dismiss the newer or smaller websites. Employers will pay more attention to candidates from new sources as they evaluate the website's effectiveness. Keep track of your online information and remember to update all your accounts at the same time.

Chapter 7: 7 Tools HR Uses to Cut You

IT'S AN UNCOMFORTABLE TRUE: HR does control quite a bit of your fate.

In fact, HR doesn't actually hire anyone. It's their job to CUT YOU. They aren't mean or against you personally, but they are required to eliminate 90%–95% of the candidates before sending their recommended people to the hiring manager. Consider this: if a job ad pulls 100–300 applicants, only 5 to 10 of them will get an in-person interview – and 10 is quite generous, by the way. That means that only 5% of job seekers *at best* earn their interviews by applying to the HR department and then praying for a miracle. See why we need to reach out to hiring managers as well?

Another hard truth: Many times, even qualified applicants will be cut during the screening process, just because they didn't understand how the hiring process works. From a lack of appropriate keywords in the resume to failing to send a cover letter when requested, these are all essential details that cost even the best potential employees the chance for a wonderful job.

Every HR department will rely on several universal tricks to weed out the candidate pool. However, once you are conscious of these tricks, they are easy to overcome.

Screening starts before you apply

One of the first problems with the process starts with the job description itself. This document will become the basis of the screening and scoring material, but many of them do not reflect the real needs of the job.

How does that happen?

Ideally, the hiring manager works closely with the HR department to create the job description, devoting time to pinpoint their ideal candidate. In practice, most job descriptions are thrown together haphazardly. The hiring manager is too busy to consult with HR. The HR department adds pieces to fit their format, regardless of the hiring manager's priority. It is a flawed system, sometimes creating a tug-of-war between managers and HR.

Some job descriptions are merely resurrections of an old description and may not reflect current needs. Some job descriptions are very vague, making it hard to guess what the employer really wants. For example, sales jobs are notorious for lacking detail, relying on nebulous terms like, "Seeking a persuasive, positive salesperson with a drive to succeed." That doesn't really help a job seeker craft a resume that would accurately address the employers' needs. On the flip side, a job description may seem like a wish list, asking for an impossibly huge skill set. In that case, the company is "feeling out" a talent pool. They may have many needs, and depending on the applicants, they will alter the actual job to match their top candidate.

Job descriptions are created in three ways:
1.   The old job description is resurrected.
The hiring manager may read over it to approve it, or she may not. Either way, it is doubtful that this description reflects current needs. This is especially a problem with IT positions. The hiring manager may add the latest desired programs or hardware, but they don't tell HR which ones to remove. Since HR doesn't fully understand what the programs are, and they don't want to eliminate something that is potentially important, the technical skills just continue to grow, all while adding more and more screening keywords into the document.

2.   The hiring manager starts a framework.

The manager may have a general idea of what he wants and then gives a draft to the HR department. From there, the HR department puts it into "their format." Often, they add unnecessary criteria, such as an education level requirement. One of the reasons for doing so is to scare off some of the applicants, which makes screening easier down the road.

3.   The hiring manager gives a wish list.

Opposite of the skimpy description, a manager may list every single aspect he would want covered. These are often long descriptions, with a seemingly impossible mix of skills. HR won't tell him to make it smaller; their goal is to get the ad placed and start drawing candidates as soon as possible.

Beware of purple squirrels

What the heck is a purple squirrel?

Born in the Great Recession of 2008, a new creature emerged on the employment landscape: the infamous purple squirrel (also sometimes referred to as "the unicorn.") The term was coined by HR departments to describe someone who has skills and experience in a wide variety of areas, such as the Executive Assistant who also does the company's IT and Marketing for the company.

Purple squirrels were created by companies as they cut their staff during the economic downturn. Rather than hire more people or contractors, they began to lean on their remaining staff to "pick up the slack" and help in other areas. Hence why the administrative assistant is now in charge of maintaining the website...

The problem arises when the purple squirrel leaves. Now the employer is looking for someone with that weird skill set mix. They really don't want to hire two people; they want a candidate who can do it all. Unfortunately, this is really hard to find. The odd job mix was based on their specific situation. So, what are the options?

Two things happen: they either hire one person who has the essential core skills and train them in the supplemental job functions; or they hire a lower-level employee and train an existing employee to pick up the other area of responsibility.

If you see a job description that asks for a bizarre mix of experience or skills, just keep in mind that they are hunting for a purple squirrel... and, by the way, most of these critters left that job because of serious burn-out from doing two jobs at once without earning a salary that would make it worth their while. Just be sure that you can accept those terms before getting too excited about a job.

The Seven Tools HR Uses to Cut You

1. Clear, written instructions

2. The Yes/ No factor

3. Industry Knowledge

4. Annoyance

5. Relevance

6. Difficult communication

7. Gut reaction

Cut #1 – Clear, Written Instructions

What it is:

A long list of very specific instructions on how to apply for the job.

Why they do this:

If you can't follow clear, written instructions, HR does not want to talk to you.

How to pass:

Send them everything they ask for, in exactly the way they request it.

Quicksand Mortality Rate: +50%

More than 50% of job seekers will be eliminated for failing to follow the directions.

The first test in any application process is to see if you can follow clear, written instructions. The HR thought process is "if you can't follow written directions, I don't want to talk to you." Passing the test is simple – send them everything they ask for, in the way they tell you to send it. Seem simple enough? You would be shocked at how many people fail this test!

Sometimes these instructions are understood, instead of formally written. For example, writing "see resume" on an application that asks for a detailed description of your duties and achievements within a particular role is NOT following the instructions. You need to copy and paste that information into their forms so that it can be searched within their database. No wonder an average application takes up to 45 minutes to complete!

How to send it

Most commercial employment websites encourage you to use the "Apply Now" button to submit your resume. Read the ad carefully – there may be a secondary email address or link hiding in the job posting itself. In that case, send a separate email to that address. Check for a name as well; addressing the cover letter to the person shows that you are detail-oriented.

Should you use the "Apply Now" feature?

This depends on where you found the job posting AND what it says to do. For example, using your LinkedIn profile to apply for a job has become very popular for employers, to the point where they will have an "Apply with LinkedIn" button on their own website. In this case, feel free to use that link.

As for other websites like Monster, CareerBuilder, or Indeed, then yes – if there is no other option. Remember the safety tips for rooting out scam jobs online: double-check the company's website to make sure the posting is legit. If you don't see it on their Careers page, just be cautious about how much information you send through the "Apply Now" button or link.

Online applications

Some companies will re-direct the candidates to their website to fill out an online application, known as the Applicant Tracking System (ATS).

It can be time-consuming and tedious. However, it is necessary. This is definitely a test of your patience as much as your ability to fill out a form. Depending on the company, you may need to list every one of your skills, along with proficiency level. If you want to get past a computerized screening process, **you must fill out those details.**

Unfortunately, many people make mistakes in the online forms. One that people often miss involves uploading your Word document. The application system will scan your resume and fill in the information on their forms – a process known as "parsing." It is not uncommon for computers to incorrectly parse your resume. Take your time and double-check your work, correcting any false computer assumptions. If there are sections requiring lots of new information, type your answers in Word first, then copy and paste your answer after you perform a spell-check.

Everyone knows that ATS applications are a horrible way to apply for a job. Chances are, if you are filling out an online application, the computers will screen you before a human even sees your resume. For this reason, online ATS are the epitome of the "HR Black Holes:" resumes come in, but they don't go out.

Another potential danger hinges on how well HR set up their system in the first place. Taleo, for example, is an ATS program that many companies use. However, when they purchase it, it is an out-of-the-box solution. If the company wants to customize it, they need to pay Taleo additional money or get their IT department to invest the time. Not all companies have those resources. One classic example of this problem was a client of mine who was transitioning out of HR. In her case, she did part of the recruitment for a major university in the Eastern US. When they got their new ATS, she oversaw setting it up and integrating it into their processes. However, about three months after the new system was implemented, she noticed that all the new hires had last names starting in A, B, C, or D. Turns out, she assumed that the ATS was delivering the screened candidate list in order of the best match, when in fact, it was alphabetical.

See why you need to track down hiring managers? Contacting the hiring authority can override a bad screening situation like this.

But no matter how annoying the application itself is, you can't skip this step. If you succeed in reaching the hiring manager but fail to fill out the online application, you can be cut for not follow instructions. Plus, the application is a legal document; if you don't fill it out, you did not legally apply for the job.

Are Cover Letters Still Necessary?

In the fall of 2017, the Personal Touch Career Services conducted a survey of HR professionals in the Denver area. The results were clear: 50% felt cover letters were helpful, 10% just use them as a screening tool (meaning that they see if it was sent, but don't read the content), and 40% felt that they were not important at all – to the point that they didn't allow candidates to upload a cover letter during the application process.

By comparison, 90% of employers and recruiters will look at your LinkedIn profile.

In many ways, LinkedIn is taking over the cover letter. And not just for small companies; large outfits such as Lockheed Martin now use LinkedIn as a viable option to apply on their own website.

What is the ultimate test? If they request the cover letter in the job posting, you better send it. No ifs, ands, or buts. Even a bad cover letter that says, "Please see my attached resume. Thank you for your consideration" is better than nothing. It at least meets their screening requirement.

With that being said, I do encourage you to write and submit a GOOD cover letter whenever you can. Even if the ATS doesn't allow it, make the cover letter the first page of your resume and send it that way. While HR may not care, hiring managers do respond to well-written letters.

If you are emailing the HR department or the hiring manager directly, put your cover letter in the body of your email. You don't need to attach it separately.

References

If they request references in the job posting, send them. Writing "references available on request" on your resume does not count – everybody has references on request. If this requirement is in the ad, *they did request your references.*

You can include your references on your resume instead of using a separate document. Including references on the resume itself ensures that you won't forget them later. Moreover, adding them to the resume overcomes an ATS, which doesn't have a section for references – even when the company asks for references. If send your references as part of your resume, their delivery is guaranteed, no matter what the delivery method.

If you're nervous about confidentiality issues, put a stipulation directly on your reference sheet:

> *"As my employment search is confidential, please do not contact my references without my permission."*

This creates a legal responsibility on the employers' part. If they contact your references and it endangers your current job, they could be held liable.

Usually, no employer is going to take the time to contact your references before they at least do a phone interview with you. It is too time consuming. References are the *last step* in the employment process, not the first. Even recruitment agencies don't check references until they are certain of your abilities.

If unsolicited contact is still a concern for you, don't send the contact information. Just list the person's name, title, and how they know you. Then add the statement: "contact information provided on request."

When sending references, be sure to send the right ones. Always include at least three professional references. If you have some personal ones to add as well, that's fine. If they know you in some sort of work capacity, such as volunteer work, that's even better. Listing only the name of a personal reference is not helpful: also indicate their job title and how they know you. Other information for personal references, such as years known, is not required, but it can be helpful. Long associations with others demonstrate your stability, which is a desirable trait to employers.

Salary history vs. salary requirements

Your salary history states how much you earned in each and every job. A salary requirement states what you want in your next job.

If the job posting requests a salary history, should you send it?
No!

If you give your salary history, you just gave away your negotiation strength. Companies look at salary history to determine a salary offer. Many people change jobs to increase their salary by as little as 5%–7%. If the employer knows the details of your past earnings, they may offer less based on your salary history. In fact, this is one of the reasons why many states are looking to make this request illegal, as it further ensures wage disparity between male and female workers.

On the other hand, you may be seeking considerably less than what you earned previously, such as if you are changing industries or transitioning into a new career path. An employer may not believe you when they see the full salary history. You are cut because your desired salary doesn't seem logical to the HR person.

The only exception to the salary history rule is a professional salesperson, especially in commissioned positions. In that case, salary history reflects success.

So how do you apply for a job posting with a salary history request?

What they really want to know is your *salary range.*

Salary range is a screening tool. Every job has a budget, whether that amount is listed in the job posting or not. Giving your salary range lets them know your expectations. If it is not within their ballpark, they won't ask you to play.

Using salary range for screening actually helps you. If you're honest and reasonable about your expectations, you would not want to consider a job out of your ballpark anyway. Taking something below your minimum creates a losing situation for you. If the salary is way above your range, the employer's expectations may be above your abilities.

Express your salary range in the cover letter, not in the resume. This gives you the ability to adjust it for every job. Some positions are more demanding; asking for more money is reasonable. Other jobs may be on your own low end; maybe you are willing to make that monetary sacrifice temporarily to change careers or employers. Salary ranges in cover letters meets the HR screening requirements.

Dear Mr. Smith:

How would you describe your ideal candidate for your Executive Assistant position listed on craigslist.com? Perhaps a detail-oriented professional, with proven problem-solving skills and real-world experience? If so, I could be the candidate you seek.

In fact, I believe many aspects of my past eight years in the XYZ industry would serve your needs extremely well.

My salary range is $51,000 to $58,000, with some flexibility considering benefits. As my employment search is confidential, please contact me on my cell phone, 303-555-1212. I would love for an opportunity to discuss your needs.

Sincerely,

Diligent Applicant

Salary range can be as large as $10,000 to even $50,000 – your ideal salary should be closer to the lower end. For example, if your target salary were $110,000, an ideal range would be $115,000–$150,000. Why? Two reasons: one, your bottom is never the bare minimum you can live on; and two, their ideal hire is in the middle of their range. (Want to know more about Salary Negotiations? Check out Chapter 11: Interviewing Practices to Know Before You Go.)

Salary history: A warning

Do be very cautious about sending your salary history. Unscrupulous characters do use job postings to steal people's identities. Listing an attractive salary history could open the door to thieves. Check out the company's website before you send anything. At the very least, try to verify the email address. If a company's listing is completely confidential and you can't find any information about them, never send the salary history. If it is a legitimate job offering, wait for them to contact you before sending such a sensitive document.

IF you must send your salary history, make it a separate document. The format should follow your regular resume – jobs listed in same order and so on – but with no duties or skills listed. This way, you will never mistake your salary history for your resume:

Cut #2 – The Yes/No Factor

What it is:
Specific criteria, skills, education, or experience required to perform the job.

Why they do this:
They really do need this particular ability to succeed in this position.

How to pass:
Use the right keywords and keep critical information easy to find.

Quicksand Mortality Rate: ~20%
For any job posting, about 20% of the candidates who survived the first cut are not qualified to do the job OR the computer did not recognize that the candidate was qualified.

Some criteria are a firm requirement in the mind of the employer. Maybe it is a critical skill for the job. Perhaps it is a specific college degree. If you are missing that crucial piece, you will be rejected. There is nothing you can do to change the employer's mind on a firm requirement.

It's a drop-dead, yes or no. You either have it or you don't.

If you think about it, some of these are obvious. For example, it is impossible to get a job as a registered nurse if you don't have a nursing degree. It is highly unlikely for you to land an executive assistant position if you have never worked in an administrative support role before. Nor will a gardener be hired as the vice president of sales, no matter how good his people skills are.

But don't lose heart yet – you can't tell from looking at the job description which requirement is a yes/no factor...

Don't have everything? Apply anyway!

Ever heard that before? It is true, and here's why: in every job description, some criteria matter more than others. You cannot tell which ones are the most important by reading the ad.

Some people try to put a formula to this, such as "the skill listed first is the most important," but that's just not true. For example, education requirements are frequently first, because *that is how traditional job descriptions are written.* The hiring manager may be more interested in the skill set or experience, but you would never know from reading the job posting.

Most HR departments screen candidates on a point system. Skills, experience, or education that is more important for the job are given a higher value. Then. all the candidates who survived the first round are evaluated by how many points they score for each criterion. Those with higher scores are considered the top candidates.

Following is a real-world example for a job opening for a Programming Technician for a television station. For this example, the requirements are listed in the same order as the job posting. In this case, the first three criteria are not the most important ones, which is why they have a lower point assignment. Notice the ones with the least amount of value:

CRITERIA SHEET Programming Technician Total Points = 100	
10	College Graduate
20	2 years of Broadcast industry experience
5	Must be available on-call during station broadcast hours
25	Ability to work with figures, especially on timing information
20	Prior experience with data entry
5	Familiarity with broadcasting operations and procedures
10	Ability to deal with a variety people with tact and efficiency
5	Must possess valid driver's license and be insurable through the company's insurance

When I was recruiting for this position, I tried to get family and friends to apply, but they refused because they didn't know broadcast operations, or they were not available to be on-call. However, those two points were the ones that *mattered least*. The employers knew the new hire would need training, so they weighted the aptitude criteria heavier.

For every job, some criteria are more important than others. Don't screen yourself out. Apply to any job that captures your attention and leave the screening to the HR department.

Review multiple job postings to find the drop-dead requirements

While you can't tell for sure what the drop-dead requirements are in a single job description, looking at a large sample can clue you in. If you keep seeing a requirement repeating in every single job posting, it is probably an absolute necessity. If you notice the exact same wording repeated in almost every ad, it is a serious requirement.

For example, with human resources (HR) jobs, unless a candidate carries a specific human resources degree with current certifications, the career options are limited. Why? Laws are constantly changing, and a top HR director must be extremely well versed in all the employment issues and changing requirements. Just as you wouldn't trust a surgeon without a license, a company will not trust their critical human resources functions to someone without a degree.

If you are serious about a career path and you know you are missing a critical degree, certification, or skill, go get educated.

Cut #3 – Industry Knowledge

What it is:
Proper use of jargon, language, acronyms – this also includes grammar and spelling errors.

Why they do this:
This is the first test to see if you know what you're doing.

How to pass:
Check your work before sending any resume or cover letter. This includes reading it out loud to check the grammar and language.

Quicksand Mortality Rate: 5%-10%
Yes, people really do use resumes, LinkedIn profiles, and cover letters with mistakes on them. Gasp!

An uneducated or inexperienced candidate often misuses common industry jargon. Letters transposed in licensing acronyms, misinterpreted duties, and badly written descriptions of their experience are all clues to the HR department. This is a sure-fire way to get cut. Nobody wants to put a sub-par candidate in front of the hiring manager. It reflects poorly on the HR department. Double-check your terminology to make sure you're on track.

If you are part of a highly technical or specialized industry, jargon becomes even more important. For example, I did some recruiting for the biodiesel industry – it's a renewable energy source that uses plant oils or animal fats to make diesel fuel for trucks and other vehicles. In searching for an engineer, we looked for someone who knew how to use the word "transesterification." (It's the bio-chemical process that turns the fats into fuel, by the way.) Any engineer in bio-diesel worth his salt knows what this means – which is why it was such a great screening term for us.

Grammar and spelling errors are death on any resume. It's even worse if you claim to be "detail-oriented" and you misspell the company's name. Pay attention to the names of people in the target company; a misspelled name screams sloppy work. Look out for casual writing. While you want to sound human, being overly familiar can be offensive.

Even your documents need to have a professional title. Make sure they have your name and job title in the Word document name, such as "Jane Smith HR Director Resume.doc" instead of "Resume Draft 2.doc." HR departments receive literally hundreds of resumes every day. If your document doesn't include your name, chances are pretty high that it might get misplaced. Any error that occurs is your fault, not theirs.

The proper use of acronyms is very important. For example, one of my clients was a Certified Nursing Assistant (CNA), but on her resume, the automated spellcheck had corrected it to "CAN." When we fixed this error, she began to get interviews the next week.

When using an acronym, be sure to write out the meaning and then the letters the first time the term is used – such as Applicant Tracking System (ATS). This is for two reasons: one, HR may not understand the acronym; and two, some companies will screen on the complete term instead of the acronym. If you have both at least once, you are less likely to get screened out because of a keyword issue.

Cut #4 – Annoyance

What it is:
If you are annoying, HR will find an excuse to cut you.

Why they do this:

Three reasons: it can be a power trip, an easy cut, or they just don't want to work with jerks.

How to pass:

Be clear and concise in all communications. Respect their time. Be professional at every turn.

Quicksand Mortality Rate: 5%-10%

Annoying people are rarely hired.

If you really get on the HR department's nerves, they will search through your resume to find the one mistake to cut you – or they may even invent one. At the screening level, HR people have a lot of power. Screening is conducted with minimal oversight, especially in the early rounds. In other words, they can cut you without fear of reprisal. This is even more reason for you to get directly in contact with the hiring managers. If they call HR and tell them to look for your resume, their actions can resurrect you from the cut candidate pile.

No phone calls, please...

In most cases, the HR department does *not* mind if you call, as long as you are not pushy or annoying. Calling to verify information is acceptable, so long as you keep it minimal. You might call to verify that a position is open, especially if the job posting is over two weeks old. However, don't call with the mindset that you want to find out specifics about the job. Some people use this excuse to "see if they want to apply." HR departments hate that. Apply first, and then make judgments about the company during an interview.

The best time to call is after you have emailed your resume or applied online. Ask three very specific questions:

1. Did you get my application?
2. Did you get the attached resume?

3.   Are you able to open it and read it properly?

If they did not get it or if they weren't able to open any uploaded documents, be sure to ask what format would work best, including the preferred email as well as Word or PDF. After you get those questions answered, you can ask other questions, but don't ask for an interview (that's very annoying.) Don't show up at the office, resume in hand and expect someone from HR to come to the front desk to see you (that's even more annoying.)

You do want to ask questions that relate to the HR person's job, such as volume of applicants. This works because people do enjoy talking about themselves.

Acceptable questions include:

1.   Have you gotten a large response?
2.   Will you be sending out notifications when the job closes?
3.   When do they anticipate holding interviews?
4.   Do you have other openings at your company?

If they are getting annoyed, be polite and end the call as soon as possible.

If you only get their voice mail, be courteous with your message, but don't expect them to call you back. A good department will still make note that you called.

Don't hound the HR department. If they don't return your phone call, be patient. They are probably very busy. Try following up with an email instead. Follow-through and making contact are positive traits, but don't call every day, nor should you send an email every day. It's ok to be interested, but don't let it slide into creepy stalking behavior.

ATS verification

You can call the HR department if you filled in the online application, just to make sure they received it. However, if you are having trouble with the system and want to get help, you will probably have minimal success. Many HR people don't want to walk you through the application because it's part of their test.

There may be something wrong with their system, such as a critical error. Treat this very carefully. HR hates calls that point out flaws in their system. They know they have flaws; they just don't want to hear it from *you*.

Again, this is another reason why you don't want HR to control your fate. Get in touch with the hiring managers.

Multiple submissions

If a company has multiple openings, send a fresh resume and cover letter for each position, clearly stating the desired job. Saying, "please consider me for anything you feel I qualify for" is absolutely horrible. Guess what they think you're qualified for? Nothing. Be confident and tell them what you want. It's not their job to help you or to be your career counselor. It's their job to cut you.

Watch your mouth

Be careful about what you say to anyone in the company. Sounds obvious, right? You would be surprised at the number of people who get mouthy with the receptionist. Guess who talks to the receptionist? Hiring managers and HR. It's a common practice for the interviewers to ask the receptionist how you behaved in the lobby. Many front-runners have lost the job based on ill manners to the front desk. Always remember that the receptionist is your doorway to the job offer or to the rejection pile.

Candidates can make fatal mistakes just by calling the main number in the wrong frame of mind. In one case, I was covering the front desk for our receptionist's lunch hour. I got a call from a job seeker who asked for me by name. The conversation went something like this:

> *Job Seeker: Can I speak to Donna Shannon?*
>
> *Me: I'm sorry, she is away from her desk right now. Would you like her voice mail?*
>
> *Job Seeker: Ugh! That Donna is so unprofessional and she's never at her desk. I've left her messages and she never calls me back. Does she even do any work around there?*
>
> *Me: Well, I can't comment on that, but I could take a message if you prefer...*
>
> *Job Seeker: No (snorts angrily.) Just give me the voice mail.*

When I got back to my desk, I eagerly checked my messages...

> *Job Seeker's voice mail: (stated sooo sweetly) Hi, Donna! This is So-N-So again. I just wanted to call and see when we could set up an interview for the Communications Assistant job...*

Well, she did get an instant response from me. I not only looked up her resume for this job but made a note in the master ATS to *never* contact her for a job again. And, before you think I'm heartless, she had only left one other voicemail before. However, when I asked the receptionist if she recognized the person, the job seeker had been making multiple calls to me, but rarely left a message.

There really is a blacklist at every company. Make sure you don't end up on it.

Cut #5 – Relevance

What it is:
They are FINALLY reading your resume for content.

Why they do this:
NOW HR is looking for the right fit, not just cutting candidates.

How to pass:

Relevance applies to more than just the job posted. It includes your research on the company while emphasizing your strengths.

Quicksand Survival Rate: 10%

Congratulations on making it to the short stack of desirable candidates.

By now you know the importance of using the right keywords and jargon. It cannot be stressed enough. If HR is scratching their heads trying to determine why you applied for a job, you lost.

Integrate your research about the company into your cover letter. Make sure your submitted materials stay on target to prove that you are the best candidate. Each job contains unique elements. A stock resume and cover letter may get you past the first level of screening, but that doesn't mean you will make the top 10%.

Believe it or not, there are actually candidates who do not read the company's website before they apply. Taking even a few moments to customize a cover letter and resume to the specific company can make a real difference. In Chapter 11: Resume Tweaking Made Easy, I do cover this in-depth.

Remember, relevance is NOT about YOU – it is about the company's needs. Consider

- What challenges are in the industry?
- What problems can you solve?
- How can you generate or save money?

All your extra work will rocket you into the final rounds.

Cut #6 – Difficult Communication

What it is:
If they have trouble reaching you, you may get cut.

Why they do this:
There are too many applicants. Due to short deadlines, they are just too busy to wait for you.

How to pass:
Answer your phone! If you can't do that, be professional and be responsive.

Quicksand Mortality Rate: Depends on how good your competition is.
The more responsive you are, the better your chances.

These are the lucky dogs who are actually getting called for a telephone interview. But that doesn't mean you're in the clear yet...

The screening process continues when the HR department starts calling candidates. One test involves how long it takes you to return their phone call. The top picks are called first, but if they must leave a message, they do keep calling other candidates.

If you don't call back within a day, you might miss your chance. If they are really interested, they may call you again. However, no HR department will call the candidate a third time without a return phone call. At that point, they have moved on to someone who was more receptive.

In your cover letter, be sure to tell them the best number and time to call. This helps alleviate some of the communication barriers. However, action is required on your part to answer the calls.

Professional communication is more than just answering the phone. Often, this is the first point where a recruiter notices that weird email address. I have seen recruiters move a candidate to the bottom of the pile because the email was suggestive or offensive.

Believe it or not, I have also seen candidates leave their phone number off their resume. In some cases, it might be acceptable to leave your street address off and only include your city and state, but nobody hunts down the candidate who didn't provide a phone number. As a tip, be sure to include your full contact information in your cover letter. This helps combat the problem of lost documents such as resumes.

Voicemail greetings can be a major problem. All too often, a recruiter hears a message that starts with "hey, dude, I can't get the phone, but leave a message..." Or worse, some rap or heavy metal song. Another greeting recruiters hate is the "voicemail lady," with the generic message that only repeats the phone number called and not the name of the account holder.

Be sure to list your name on your greeting. Recruiters get antsy when they aren't sure about who they are talking to.

Cut #7 – Gut Reaction

What it is:
Before sending any candidate to the hiring manager, HR weighs all the factors. Those who have a positive experience move forward.

Why they do this:
Every candidate put before a hiring manager reflects HR's work.

How to pass:
Be relevant, professional and passionate.

Quicksand Survival Rate: Only 3%-5% of all applicants
Remember, these are *survivors,* not necessarily the *best qualified.*

When the candidate list is narrowed to the top picks, instinct plays a part. The best HR recruiters and hiring managers often choose to call one candidate over another because "it feels right."

Hiring people is a risk and employers are cautious. They want to feel confident in a person's abilities, even before they pick up the phone for the first contact. If you keep your materials professional, accurate, and relevant, these subconscious feelings will react to your presentation. You appear to be someone who knows what they are doing. That's the instinct pull they are looking for, the ability to put them at ease.

All the extra homework on researching the company pays off here. During your phone interview, be sure to ask relevant and intelligent questions.

Confidence comes across on paper. Self-respect is a tangible element in the job search, and it shows in the way you write and speak about yourself. Most employers want someone who is competent and interested in their specific job, not just "any old job." That's the "spark," the "magic bullet" that pierces the corporate veils.

 Finally, be sure to send a thank you note to the HR people for any interview – including a phone interview. While most candidates remember to thank a hiring manager, very few send thanks to a recruiter. This can help tip scales in your favor.

Be conscious of the tips and tricks HR uses to cut you and you will consistently be in the top 5%.

Final words on dealing with HR

Now that you know how the HR department is screening you, you never have to fall victim to these tricks. Remember to follow their rules, even the unspoken ones. Be professional and complete in all your communications. Use your tools from this book to make sure you are in the top 5% of any candidate field.

Chapter 8: Essential Organization and Research Tools

Whether you are researching a company to unveil the potential for a hidden job or checking out the employer because they just posted an opening, organizing your materials and conducting accurate research is a major focus of your job search.

First, make a list of companies that *could* be interesting to you. These may be places that you already know, such as large companies in your area or a firm that just posted a new job. At first, the list may have only 10–20 businesses on it, but our overall goal is to identify 100 over the course of your job search.

IMPORTANT: this is a _Prospecting_ list. Don't run out and start researching the companies immediately. You just want to add them to the list if you would be interested in learning more about them. Once you have some companies on the list, sort them by your A, B, and C choices, with A's being your top interest, B's those that seem ok, and C's are, well, something that you might want to just throw your resume into the ring to see what happens.

Every week, you will be picking out 5-10 target employers, plus any new posted jobs you may find. Once identified, you will do research to qualify them to see if they are really a good fit for you.

Remember, the last thing you want to do is immediately start filling out an application the moment you see a job posted. Not only could this waste your time because the application itself may take 45 minutes, you also failed to research the company to see if they were really a place where you want to work. Even worse, taking this shotgun approach to your job search – just shooting blindly into the dark and hoping that something hits – frequently are less productive than sending the targeted, researched resumes. That may sound counterintuitive, but you will gather more results doing an excellent job on 10 applications per week vs. frantically applying to 50 jobs in the same timeframe.

Remember, QUALIFYING is a crucial step in your sales process, saving you hours of wasted time in pursuing opportunities that are really a bad fit for you. Take the time to separate your prospecting from your qualifying research to focus and streamline your efforts.

Sometimes your research will be quick. A 10-minute perusal of the company's reputation on Glassdoor.com or Google may show you way more dirt and bad attitudes than you would ever want in your work environment. Or maybe they just announced that their headquarters is moving to Canada. Or maybe their CEO was just indicted for embezzlement or fraud. Great! Don't waste your time on these guys anymore. Move on to the next prospect on the list or the next posted job.

So, what exactly are you trying to find out? Basically, everything that you can – especially the pieces that relate to your overall job goals. Obviously, you want to start by reaching their website and determining the basics, such as their mission, products, services, and leaders. Check out the careers page not only for open jobs but also insight into their process or hiring trends. Not only that, some of the common job boards like Indeed are a breeding ground for scam jobs, designed to steal your identity. If you conduct an independent search the company's website rather than just following the "Apply Now" link, you can reveal these scams.

If you are still interested in the company after learning the basics, start expanding that search to fill in the gaps. First, look for any reviews. Just like restaurants are reviewed on Yelp, employment sites like Indeed and Glassdoor are pushing for employee reviews to give insight into working for the company. Of course, it's anonymous, so take it with a grain of salt. But if the trends run universally negative, take heed.

Start forming a profile for that employer. This includes their mission, core services and products, clients they serve, size, industry, history, and other facts that are important to you.

Possible topics are:

- Company history, products and services

- Key managers/ players and support staff

- Competitors

- Growth plans and challenges

Organizing Your Prospecting and Qualifying Efforts

Since the job search itself is a sales process, it is important to implement some way to track your progress and organize all this information that you will be gathering. In business, this is done through a central software hub known as the CRM, or Customer Relationship Management, program. For job seekers, this can be as complex or as simple as you want to make it. What is essential is that you have a system that you consistently use to track key information which includes specific action items to keep you moving forward.

Simple Systems

First and foremost, create a spreadsheet of your target companies, which will be your Master Prospecting List. This is for the most basic information, such as the company name, contact information, date added to the list, date researched, and if they have any current job postings. Be sure to have fields for follow-up dates AND when they are performed. The idea is that when you look at your list, you can immediately see what opportunities need immediate action.

Next, create folders – either physical or on your computer – for each one of your target companies. Usually, you would do this once they have "passed" your first level of research; in other words, if you still are interested in learning more after the 10-minute review of their website and reputation, you should start documenting them.

	Prospect #1 (Example)	Prospect #2
Company	Personal Touch Career Services	
City, State	Westminster, CO	
Website	www.personaltouchcareerservices.com	
Phone Number	720-452-3400	
Industry	Consulting/Career Coaching	
Main Products or Services	Job Search Assistance	
Contact	Donna Shannon	
Email	donna@personaltouchcareerservices.com	
Priority (A, B, C)	A	
Follow Up Date		
Notes		

Detailed Company Information

Now, develop a Company Page Word template that you will use for each and every company. This is where you will document your critical information from your research. While your Master Prospecting List includes just the basics, your Company Page is where you will be capturing the details. It is meant to be a living document that expands as you learn more about the company. Don't be tempted to print it off and write this stuff by hand; in many cases, you will be capturing live website links.

Don't forget to save your Company Pages in a consistent format so you can find them later. For example, ABC Company may have the file name "ABC Company Denver 2019.docx" under a file of the same name – and yes, it is a good idea to always date your work.

Company Prospecting

Company Info
Name:
Full Adress:
Website:
Phone Number(s):
Linkedin Page:
Other Social Media:

Contacts Info

C-Level and Executive Leadership
(include email and LI profile):
Top Managers in my area:
Other key employees or peers:
HR Contacts:
Contacts I already have there:
Where are jobs posted?:

Other Info

Date founded/history:
Company size (employee count):
Revenue Range:
Key Products or Services:
Competitors:
Notes:

Tracking Job Openings

Another crucial document is the Job Openings template. Any time you see a job posted at your target company, you need to document both your actions and your research. You should have a different page for each job opening at the target company. Remember to save the posting date in your file name, which will help you see the most recent postings without having to open the document, such as "20190101Executive Assistant ABC Company." This formula indicates that the job was posted on January 1, 2019. By putting the YEAR – MONTH – DAY, your documents within the company folder will be automatically sorted by date. This helps when you want to identify future follow-ups based on the position's posting date.

Notice that we do want to include the full job posting on this document. Online job posts frequently expire before the interviews start, so capture that information before it disappears.

Job Opening

THE
Personal Touch
CAREER SERVICES

Company:

Job Listing url:

Date Posted:

Date Applied:

Resume &
Cover Letter Used (file name):

Follow Up Dates:

Key Managers:

Contact Info:

Date Contacted:

Results:

Full Job Description (copy/paste):

Online Systems

While it's true that you can do a lot to track your progress using MS Office or similar tools, more advanced users may actually want to use an online CRM system. Many of these can even be managed through your mobile device, once the initial set-up is done. While not a requirement, it can be a convenient way to keep all your research, tracking, and next step reminders in one place.

Many of these cloud-based CRMs have relatively inexpensive monthly rates, designed to appeal to small businesses. Depending on how much you want to invest, you can get CRMs that are integrated with many news sources. Following are some examples, as well as their relative price ranges as of 2019 (subject to change, as they are independent.)

	Hunter	Discover Org	Info Free	Crunchbase
Website	hunter.io	discoverorg. com	infofree.com	crunchbase. com
Claim to Fame	Google extension	For sales, marketing, and recruiting	Multiple databases	Contacts + business news
Feature	100 free emails/month	Verified and refined data	25 contacts/ day visable	Wide reach on business
Best	1,000 requests monthly, affordable	Cross referenced data, beautiful	Holds 500 online contacts	Export lists, free tools
Worst	Focus on emails on public site	Annual subscription only	Setup can be complex	Bill annually for discount ($29/month)
Cost (monthly)	$39	$25, 000 (yearly)	$49	$49
Setup Fee	$0	$0	$99	$0

Want to see more? Check out: https://www.tenfold.com/sales-prospecting/big-list-40-prospecting-tools-modern-salesperson/

One interesting thing to note about this: I bet you saw Discoverorg.com on the list. Yes, this is one of the most comprehensive recruiter re-searching tools and CRM/ATS in the market. Not only does it track news from outside sources, the company actually calls the top cor-porations on a regular basis to learn about when senior leaders are being promoted or leaving. Yep, it's the best – and no, that price tag of $25,000 A YEAR is not a typo!

So, who in their right mind is paying for that? The top executive recruiters and headhunters, of course. They will easily make that back on just one placement, with plenty of room to spare. People ask me all the time on whether they should work with recruiters or not. THIS is why – they have resources way beyond your capacity, as well as rela-tionships with the employers that may be difficult for you to get. Even if you aren't seeking a top executive role, any recruiter builds their business by developing employer relationships that may be difficult for you to develop. Remember, leave no stone unturned!

Speaking of secret opportunities, remember to be twice a vigi-lant when tracking your information on a hidden job.

Sources for hidden jobs

Hidden jobs can come from any source – networking, following the news, tracking industry leaders, or just identifying the top-rated com-panies in terms of job satisfaction. Whatever the source, the defining factor is that you reach out to the company before they posted the job of your dreams.

So, where are these potential employers? Check out hot lists, such as the Forbes 500. Local business magazines love to generate lists as well, such as *Colorado Business Magazine's* annual Best Places to Work. Trying to target smaller employers? Don't forget such re-sources as the members of your local Chamber of Commerce.

Another great source for uncovering hidden jobs is researching hot industries in your area. Your local Economic Council and Bureau of Labor Statistics can identify the top markets. While we used to say, "do what you love, and the money will follow;" we now have the mentality of "find the money and do what you love there." For example, Colorado's Labor Market Indicator (LMI) Gateway – https://www.colmigateway.com – shows statistical information on the Top 10 Occupations and the Top 10 Employers, based on posted positions from the previous month. If you are the kind of person who just loooves statistics, there is plenty of data on the labor market profiles, data trends, and employment and wage data. Armed with this knowledge, you can explore new industries, review relevant salary information, and even check local demographics.

If you are still struggling with a specific target job, the government created a couple of interesting websites: www.MyNextMove.org and www.OnetOnline.org. Both stem from a special project by the Federal government to create a repository of all the jobs in the US. MyNextMove is more user-friendly, while OnetOnline is more comprehensive. When you search for jobs by keywords, they show you related or similar jobs – which can be very helpful in determining divergent job titles. After all, it's very difficult to find a job on Indeed or LinkedIn if you don't know the specific title of that target job. Plus, these sites show the projected growth potential of the jobs, which can be helpful when seeking a long-term position in a stable market.

In addition to your prospecting lists for companies and industries, you need a springboard for your networking efforts. Just like our company list, this doesn't mean you are going to run out the door to every one of the events. Start looking around for the opportunities and become aware of what's available in your area. Remember, social media DOES count as networking, if you use it correctly.

Some possible networking avenues include:

• Professional associations.

• Business, professional, or job seeker groups on Meetup.com.

- Casual or fun groups (plan your recess!)

- LinkedIn Groups.

- Facebook Groups.

Want more ideas? Check Appendix I: Research Resources

Trigger events

One of the best sources for research is paying attention to the news. This means internet sources, business magazines, and press releases as well as traditional print or broadcast sources. In fact, sometimes they are better, as large media can be selective about what they spread. So, how can you easily stay on top of the latest news on your target companies?

Google Alerts.

Simply set up some Google Alerts:

(https://www.google.com/alerts) These will feed you the latest news and happenings of your target company. While you do need a Google account to use the service, you can send the alerts to any email address. You can select how often you want to see them as well. Tired of following a specific target? You can delete them with one click.

So, what are you looking for? Trigger events.

Trigger events are any excuse to reach out to a hiring manager, whether there is a job opening or not. For example, they may have just won an award, landed a large contract, announced a merger, or hired a new senior leader.

Some examples include:

- Landing a new, large contract

- Expanding to a new location

- Receiving an award

- Releasing a new, innovative product

- Hiring a new CEO, VP or other top manager

- Being featured on a Top 100 Companies list

- Being interviewed by the media

- Making a large charity donation

Here lies the magic of the unadvertised job: pure anticipation of needs. Think about what kind of staff or employees they will need in the future based on these triggers. Not everyone can do this; if you are able to determine a company's needs based on current situations, it is a huge asset. Timing is another critical factor. It is not enough to be aware of the targeted employer. You must be aware of the overall industry changes, trends within your geographical area and other factors in the professional landscape.

Personally, I have gained interviews with companies for jobs that did not exist yet. One situation involved a radio station that was featured in the local news for buying several repeater stations in the mountains. (Repeaters reinforce and rebroadcast an FM radio signal to outlying areas, especially ones that would be interrupted by large geographical changes, such as mountain terrain – just in case you were wondering.) I developed a custom cover letter that specifically addressed not only their possible needs but also demonstrated my expertise in the broadcast industry. In the end, I met with the CEO, COO, and Director of Sales even though they didn't have a position available. Within a month, they formally posted a job based on my recommendations from those interviews. I interviewed one more time to make it "official," although in the end they hired a relative for the position. (Don't feel bad – they were off the air six months later, so some things do happen for a reason!)

To accomplish a successful bid for an unadvertised job, you need to roll up your sleeves and do as much research as possible. It not only lands the job, it makes it easier to be effective from the first day.

Chapter 9: Track Down the Hiring Manager

While research is the crux of your Qualifying process, Discovery is our deep-dive into that target company. Without a doubt, the very best thing you can do for your job search is to track down and contact hiring managers directly, whether there is an active job posting or not.

But how is that even possible?

Thanks to the Information Age, it is getting easier than ever before to find these decision makers AND their contact information.

Side-stepping the HR department

Believe it or not, many managers are just as frustrated with the HR department as job seekers are. They have a clear understanding of what their team needs, not just in terms of the skills set, experience, and education, but also the drive, personality, and soft skills that will fit best with their team. Unfortunately, the candidates that HR sends are not necessarily the most qualified for the job; they are the ones who survived the screening process the best.

The problem is that while HR controls the hiring process, they are a slave to it as well. Rather than considering a candidate's abilities, they must react to the words on the resume. Sometimes that means a computer is cutting the candidate before a human even reads the resume, just based on keywords alone.

For example, I was speaking to some IT professionals recently while teaching a class on resume writing. One of them pointed out that he was screened out of a job, even though he met all the qualifications. Because he knew someone at the company, he actually got feedback that he was screened out for lacking a bachelor's degree. The problem? He DID HAVE a bachelor's in Computer Science. However, the screening computer cut his resume because the job description stated, "Bachelor's degree required," and his resume said, "B.S., Computer Science."

B.S., indeed.

This kind of thing happens every day. Worse, hiring managers are losing out on qualified candidates because HR can't break from their regimented processes to weed through literally hundreds of applicants for each job posting.

Not only that, HR will often add requirements to limit the candidate field. When I used to work with a biodiesel company in Colorado, I would ask the hiring managers if a degree was required for the position. Many times, the manager would state, "I don't care, so long as the person can do the job."

Guess what I added?

Yep, that dang degree. This way, I had less candidates to consider because I scared off some of the talent pool on purpose. When I evaluated the candidates, I did put less emphasis on the degree, but many people never took the chance to apply just because they lacked that qualification.

For all these reasons and more, hiring managers are very willing to accept resumes directly from candidates. Why do you think they ask their current team to provide references for potential employees? It is far less painful to tap your current employee network than fight with an HR department that is producing less-than-ideal candidates.

The trick is to reach out to the managers, whether through a current or past employee or by contacting them directly.

However, don't blow off HR entirely. You still need to apply and prove that you can follow the written instructions in the job posting. Plus, that is how you legally apply for the job.

Finding That Name and Contact Information

Ah, what's in a name? If it is the hiring manager, it is everything! If we can find the name of the hiring manager, we can conduct further research to find their contact information. Fortunately, there are many sources to find that elusive name, including:

- The company's website

- LinkedIn company pages and direct search

- Networking groups

- Personal network

- Prospecting websites and tools

- The Company Website

Sure, this may seem overly simple, but always start with the company's website. Sometimes the job description itself will include the title of the hiring manager, like this example:

Unfortunately, most employers are not using this helpful information in their job postings. That would be too easy!

Check out the other resources on the company website to gain valuable information, including:

- Management team

- About us

- Blog posts

- News or Media Room

Even if you don't find the specific manager for your role, pay attention to the other key players. I like to check the blog posts for current marketing messages. The media pages, especially the media kit if the company has one, are treasure troves of information for the savvy job seeker.

The other reason to check the company blog or news is because you are looking for the email address patterns within the company. The Public Relations person may not be the hiring manager but using that person's same email address pattern can lead to a reasonable guess as to almost any other employee.

LinkedIn Company Pages and Direct Search

LinkedIn is your next go-to source. [Still struggling with LinkedIn? Please visit my full online course, "Using LinkedIn to Get a Job Without Going Crazy:" https://www.udemy.com/using-linkedin-to-get-a-job/?couponCode=FLYER75] While the online course covers everything in depth, let me just highlight the importance of the company pages.

Company pages are helpful because they offer not only insight to the company and its open jobs, but a direct link to a filtered search of their employees – INCLUDING indicating which ones are your 1st Degree connections.

For example, if you were to look up AT&T on LinkedIn, you would see over 200,000 employees worldwide listed. However, if you go to the company page, it may show that you have eight connections that work there. That doesn't mean that they are your only possible way to reach managers there. Use the pre-sorted employee list plus LinkedIn's filters and standard Boolean search terms to further refine the results until you see probable target managers.

If you aren't familiar with Boolean search terms, these are the different qualifiers that help define search parameters. Some of the basics are:

- " " = searches for the exact phrase of everything within the quotation marks

- AND = all terms or phrases but not the exact order

- NOT = excludes the term

- OR = results include both terms

A direct search would work in a similar way. You would just start directly from the Search fields and then use your filters and Boolean search terms to drive the results.

For example, if you narrowed your search to only "network engineer" AND manager within AT&T along with the Location filter of Denver area, the results drop to 27 potential people. By the way, LinkedIn will offer more filters if you decide to pay for a Premium account or up your membership level. I highly encourage you to become adept at the Boolean search terms to become more efficient without having to pay for LinkedIn.

Contact Information on LinkedIn

If you are lucky, your target manager will include their contact information on their profile, especially if they place it in the Summary section. However, most people don't do this, for obvious reasons. Another option is that once they accept your invitation to connect, you may be able to see their contact information – if they entered it, that is.

Usually, you need to try to make contact through LinkedIn directly and then continue to cultivate the relationship from there. Keep in mind, though, that some people are highly active on LinkedIn and will see your message or invitation. Others, however, barely check their account and have even turned off their email notifications. How can you be certain that your message will be received?

First and foremost, check your target's profile to see if they are active on LinkedIn. Here are the signs that they are a heavy LinkedIn user:

- Completeness of the profile

- Number of connections

- Number of Groups

- Published articles (if any)

- Recent activity

A complete profile means more than just having everything filled out. A heavy user will have a custom picture, a descriptive headline, and a robust summary. If they have recent activity on LinkedIn – specifically, posting articles, making comments, or "liking" other people's content – this will show up on the profile underneath the summary. If you don't see this field, it means there has been none of this type of activity for several months.

 Be sure to check out their Groups. Did you know that fellow Group members can send messages and invitations to each other for FREE? If you want to connect with someone, join the same Groups and then send the invitation.

Not sure where the target's groups are listed? They are hidden under the Interests section at the end of the profile. Click on the "see more" link at the bottom of the Interests section to see their Groups, along with what Companies they are following and any Schools.

Networking Groups

Have you ever been to a networking group for job seekers, where everyone starts with a 30-second introduction that includes their top three target companies? This is why your networking groups are part of the prospecting and discovery point of the sales process. You are hoping to find opportunities or discover more about those potential employers.

If you are extremely lucky, you will be sitting next to someone who was the college roommate of the hiring manager at your target company. Not only that, he likes you and is willing to take your resume to that manager directly. However, that probably won't happen.

A better possibility is to find either a past or current employee who can tell you more about that employer. What you want is information, not that commitment to pass your resume forward.

Sometimes people don't even realize the value of their knowledge. For example, my husband, Ryan, has worked with Johns Manville in Denver for over 15 years. He doesn't think that he has any valuable information for the job seekers. However, he knows all the key managers, the hiring process, and insight into the company culture.

Use your networking groups and guide these contacts on what you are hoping to learn from them. You will get better information – including key managers' names – when you let people know what you need.

Your Current Network

Don't forget to tap into your current network to gain that same information you wanted from the networking group members. This is exactly why you want to search for your 1st Degree connections on LinkedIn when you see a job pop up with one of your target employers. It doesn't matter if they are in a different department or if they are not a manager – you need information and they have it, even if they don't know it yet.

Prospecting Websites

Prospecting websites are like large databases that compile information on companies, both across the country and worldwide. We did touch on these as a CRM option for you in Chapter 7: Essential Organization and Research Tools, however, even if you don't use them as your core CRM, there are some helpful tools that you can use. Some do require a paid account, but there are options for free resources that are not as in-depth.

So, what kind of information are these sites gathering? While some collect overall data on the employers, such as Crunchbase.com and Mattermark.com, others are more interested in mapping the key personnel, like TheOfficialBoard.com. What is similar between all of them is that they collect *direct contact information* for many of the key employees.

The good news is that there are some more affordable options for job seekers, including some free data scrapers.

One of my favorite resources is **Hunter.io**, which is a free data scraper. You do need to know the company's official website for this to work.

When you do the search, Hunter.io shows the most common email pattern along with direct email addresses it found on the site. Further, it shows you how often that email appeared and how recently it was entered.

Don't worry if Hunter.io does not find the direct email address of your target, although you can further search through these results to possibly find that person. What is most important is identifying the email patterns. We are really lucky that IT departments are so efficient – once they set the email pattern for the company, it will be the same for almost every employee, including your target manager. Within a few tries, you should be able to guess the hiring manager's email address based on these common patterns.

Is This the Right Manager?

Another trick with tracking down managers is figuring out which one would be the hiring manager for your job. Smaller companies are easier to figure out, but large corporations may have multiple divisions that could be viable options.

Here's the secret: ALL possible managers are your target, including those in positions higher than your direct supervisor.

It works like this: say you found two potential managers for your target job, Bob Jones and Jane Smith. You send your emailed resume to both. Well, Bob is the actual hiring manager, but he deletes the email without reading it. However, Jane does open hers and realizes that Bob could use your help. She forwards the message to Bob, who now opens it because it came from a trusted coworker.

Reaching Out to Key Managers

Now that you have the name, making contact is the next big thing. However, we want to make sure they are going to receive the message correctly. This could be an InMail through LinkedIn, an invitation to connect, an email, or even an old-fashioned letter through the mail. Usually, you want to reach out in a few different ways. After all, one strategy may work great on one person and fall flat with anther.

Personally, I like to approach a high-value target on multiple fronts. I send an invitation through LinkedIn along with a direct email, followed up by a phone call a day later.

 One note of caution with this: while most companies don't mind receiving emailed resumes, you don't want to become excessive. I know of one job seeker who was adamant about working for a certain mid-sized company in the Denver area. He managed to get a full employee list, including the contact information. Every week, he sent all the managers a copy of his resume. After three months of this he did finally get a response from HR. It was a cease and desist order, stating that if he didn't stop sending the emails, they would sue him for harassment.

Best practices are to reach out to the managers no more than two times. You want to be persistent – not a huge pest.

Chapter 10: Structured Networking

Networking: the word that strikes terror into the heart of many job seekers. Instantly, the horrifying image of walking into a crowded room of 200 people springs to mind, with everyone trying to shove their business cards at each other and make a positive impression with strangers in less than five minutes.

Worse, you know you should be doing it. Everywhere, you keep hearing that 80% of open jobs are found through networking. But how can this mass hysteria possibly lead to a job?

Well, it doesn't.

Gathering in large groups and passing around business cards is the least effective way to conduct networking. In some rare cases, you might come across someone who can be of real benefit to your job search, but the fact is that most of these large-scale events rarely work. Networking is only effective when you can leverage the contacts you already have while building solid relationships with new ones.

This is the idea behind structured networking.

Just as we have a structured job search plan, structured networking uses many tactics to build on past successes while keeping the pipeline moving forward.

How Networking Works

Networking is about increasing your overall number of quality connections. NOTE: quality is always more important than quantity. I am personally connected to over 3,800 people on LinkedIn, but the majority of my leads or business referrals probably comes from a select few hundred.

Another key concept to keep in mind is that you aren't just connecting with the single person in front of you. Instead, you want to gain their trust and confidence enough that they feel comfortable sharing THEIR contacts with you. The concept is that everyone you approach, while probably not personally in control of your target job, can at least connect you to several additional people. From those contacts, you gain access to several more. If each person only passed you along to one other person, your networking efforts would be linear. Instead, a growing networking base leads to multiple further contacts from everyone, resulting in an exponential networking effort.

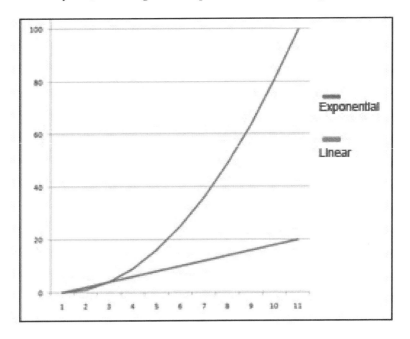

Why, you might ask, will people be willing to help me, or even talk to me in the first place? The answer is two-fold: (1) it is good business practice to try to help others, and (2) networking is a reciprocal process. Even if you can't directly assist the person who helps you out today, being an active and open participant and being available in the future keeps the lines of goodwill active. Be assured, therefore, that you are not "using" people. You are not "begging" friends and associates. You are using a relationship resource that you have been building throughout your career. Without a doubt, you will be able to help others in the future, doing your own part to "pay it forward."

 Networking isn't a quick fix to finding your next job. It's an important aspect of good business practices. With thought, sensitivity, and preparation, networking becomes a natural way to build productive, mutually beneficial professional relationships. These are the quality relationships that lead to a rich career – not just an information source.

Networking Best Practices

Unfortunately, some ill-prepared job seekers have poisoned the process because they didn't understand how to network effectively. There are cardinal sins that they thoughtlessly committed. Don't make these fatal mistakes:

- Never ask for a job – ask for suggestions.

- Don't ask for favors – ask for advice.

- Always offer something to the contact – this includes access to your own network, market insight, or even buying them coffee for their time.

- Be very conscious of their time – don't overstay your welcome or freak out if they don't respond to you right away.

- Find the way that they prefer to communicate and stick with that – whether it is through LinkedIn, email, phone, or another social media platform.

- Be grateful for any help or insight you receive – no matter how small.

If you are well-prepared and focused and apply these rules, networking will most likely work for you.

Network Levels

Every networking strategy is built on expanding both our inner networks and outer networks. Inner networks consist of the people you already know. Outer networks are comprised of the people you don't know yet. Our goal with networking is to deepen our relationships with existing networks while expanding our base in outer networks.

With each level, we start with the people closest to us and then expand outward.

INNER AND OUTER NETWORKS

Inner networks consist of the people you already know. Outer networks are comprised of the people you don't know yet. By getting comfortable with leveraging your current network, you will build confidence and be more effective when building new relationships.

INNER NETWORK: CHAMPIONS

Your Champions are the people closest to you - your family, friends, and everyone who wants to see you succeed.

INNER NETWORK: LIGHT CONNECTIONS

Light connections are people you know, but on a friendly basis. This can be past co-workers, past managers, colleagues, fellow alumni, social connections, and even relatives.

OUTER NETWORK: QUALITY TIME

Quality time means that you are meeting people in a setting that lets you get to know them and build relationships. This includes intimate networking groups, social media, and reaching out to people directly through LinkedIn or email.

OUTER NETWORK: VOLUME NETWORKING

Volume networking is all about spreading awareness about who you are. This means everything from large, after-hours events to general social media posts, like writing articles or sharing blogs on LinkedIn.

Inner Network: Champions

Your Champions are the people closest to you, who want to see you succeed and are a solid support for you. This is your family, significant other, closest friends, and even your dog. Champions provide emotional strength in the face of the often-challenging job search. They are willing to listen when you need to vent or just let off steam when the job search gets too frustrating. You know you can trust them with anything while they simultaneously act as your cheerleader and rally point.

While our Champions may want us to succeed, they don't always know what they can do for our job search, especially in terms of networking. Here's where you can help them help you. When you are up for a specific position, ask your Champions if they know anything about the company. They may even know someone from the target employer, but not even realize it. This doesn't mean a direct connection to the hiring manager. More than likely, it will be a LinkedIn connection they forgot they had, especially if they have a larger online network. Just ask them to do a search to see if they have anyone and then ask for an introduction.

 Champions genuinely want to help you. Other ways they can help is running mock interviews, reviewing your resume and LinkedIn profiles, or taking a peek at your outgoing letters. If it is your direct family or significant other, get their buy-in on your job search, meaning that they completely understand the amount of time and space the job search will actually take – time that might be taken away from them. Most of all, they are the ones who can shore you back up after getting the rejection notice after several rounds of interviewing.

Inner Network: Light Connections

Light Connections are people that you already know, but on a less intimate basis, such as an acquaintance or friend. This can be past coworkers, past managers, colleagues, fellow alumni, social connections, and even further-removed relatives.

Your Light Connections are probably more numerous than you think, as they include everyone who knows you, not just your business contacts. If it feels weird, think about it this way: people want to do business with people they know, like, and trust. The same is true when making referrals for possible jobs. One person mentioned to me that her best source for jobs was actually her quilting circle that met on a weekly basis. Over the course of hours and weeks, everyone got to genuinely know her. That type of trust leads to people feeling confident about sharing their job leads or their own network connections.

When tapping into our Light Connections, the goal is to move them into a deeper relationship or rekindle the one that was there previously. This is especially true with people that you worked with in the past. It is so easy to lose track of people as "life happens," but that is all the more reason why we should stay in touch with our network even when we aren't looking for a job.

To effectively reach out to your Light Connections, make sure that every initial message includes questions about them or a way that you can help them. Nobody really likes to be pumped for job leads from a former colleague who they haven't spoken to in years. Not sure what to say? Check out Appendix II: Networking Tools for specific suggestions based on different situations.

When identify your Light Connections, use these tools:

- Search your LinkedIn first-degree connections

- Go through your contacts in your email

- Ask your Champions about additional people to contact, such as relatives

Outer Network: Quality Time

Our first level in the Outer Networks is the Quality Time designation. As an Outer Network, these are people who don't know you yet. Quality time means that you are meeting them in a setting that allows you to actually get to know them better. This includes smaller networking groups, association meetings, social media, and reaching out to people directly through LinkedIn or email.

The best thing about these Quality Time situations is that it leads to real, professional relationships while also spreading your brand awareness. For example, I encourage people to join job seeker networking groups in your area, ideally ones that meet on a monthly or weekly basis. Because you see people over and over, they become more comfortable with sharing their network with you.

Social media is a great avenue for building relationships with new people. In particular, I find getting involved in groups – whether in LinkedIn or Facebook – can be beneficial, as everyone is interested in the same topic. By sharing quality content and making remarks to ongoing discussions, you can become known for sharing quality content on a consistent basis. But just breeding good will is not enough. You must take it to the next level.

When you are fellow group members with someone on LinkedIn, you can actually send them a message or invite them to connect with you without paying for a LinkedIn Premium account.

Quality Time networking also involves reaching out directly to decision makers at your target companies. Even if there is not a job opening at the time, conducting informational interviews is a great way to find out more about the company and this person. You can use informational interviews to contact the people that your Champions or Light Connections suggested as well.

Whatever the original source, the most important piece for a Quality Time networking effort is following up. You don't want to devote a ton of time into tracking down people, attending groups, or posting in social media if you don't do something to maintain contact. Your goal is to move these Quality Time events into Light Connections – or, even better, Champions.

Outer Network: Volume Networking

Finally, Volume Networking for the Outer Networks consists of reaching many people at once. It is all about spreading awareness about who you are. This means everything from large, after-hours events and job fairs to general social media posts, like writing articles or sharing blogs on LinkedIn.

For example, I do a lot of posting content within my LinkedIn groups, both articles that I wrote myself and other interesting articles

I found. After having done this on a consistent basis for several years, I do get recognized a lot. It is not uncommon for me to attend a national convention and have people walk up to me and state, "I know you from somewhere..." When I reply, "LinkedIn?" They immediately jump and say, "yep, that's it!"

Volume Networking can also be considered as a form of broadcasting. When a message goes out on the radio or on Twitter, it is accessible to everyone. All they have to do is tune in or follow the hashtag. By contrast, Quality Time is like sending direct emails or snail mail to a person. It's more intimate and specific to that person's needs.

 Volume Networking is not about reaching a single person; however, it lays the foundation for why someone would want to connect with you. Remember how all your networking efforts need to lead back to what we have to offer other people? Sharing your thoughts, forwarding articles, recognizing key people in your industry, and even introducing people to each other at a large networking event all ties back to be a valuable resource.

Be a giver, not a taker.

See Appendix II: Networking Tools to track your progress and see suggestions for networking messages.

Chapter 11: Tweaking Your Resume

Before we get started, let me be perfectly clear: **this chapter is NOT about writing a resume from scratch.** It will address taking a solid resume and tweaking parts of it to fit a specific position. If you still need to write a solid resume, STOP RIGHT NOW and read my other book, *"How to Get a Job Without Going Crazy (2nd Ed.)."*

Realize this fact as well: in most cases, it is not necessary to completely revise your resume for every job that you apply to. The deciding factor is how strict the HR ATS screening computers are and how regimented the company's hiring practices are. For example, anything with the federal government is going to require heavy customization to the resume and supplemental documents, because they also ask for in-depth essay answers to questions.

If you are going for two different types of jobs – say, HR and accounting or network engineer and technical sales – those need different base resumes from the get-go. It takes a lot more work to make an HR resume tweak out for accounting, or to adjust a heavy technical network engineer resume into a sales position that requires more people skills.

Save yourself some insanity by always starting with good, targeted resumes before adjusting for specific companies or roles.

Who is your audience?

Depending on who you are sending your resume to, you need to take different factors into consideration. Different people (or screening computers) care about different parts of your resume. What is perfect for the HR department may be less impressive to a hiring manager or

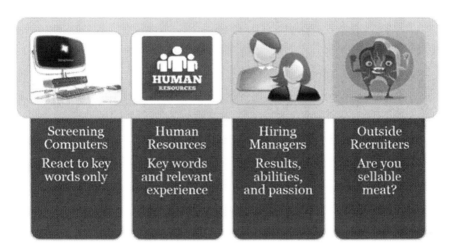

Screening Computers	Human Resources	Hiring Managers	Outside Recruiters
React to key words only	Key words and relevant experience	Results, abilities, and passion	Are you sellable meat?

outside recruiter.

Screening Computers, aka Applicant Tracking System or ATS

Any time you upload your resume into an online application, chances are that you will be screened by a computer before a human being ever sees the document. Computers rely heavily on the keywords within the job description to determine if a candidate is qualified or not. Unfortunately, this includes both smart and "stupid" keywords.

Smart keywords are terms that directly relate to the job or qualifications, such as names of specific computer programs that need to be mastered to do the job effectively. This also includes years of experience, specific college degrees, or even vital personality traits like entrepreneurial spirit or cross-functional team leadership.

Stupid keywords are the phrases that we all hate, usually because they are cliché or don't really mean anything anymore. Do you hate the phrase "excellent communication skills?" We all do! But if HR continues to use these phrases in their job descriptions, we MUST use them somewhere in the resume or risk being screening out by the computer because you are not qualified.

In general, computers need a **60-70% match on keywords alone** to forward a resume on to the real, live people in the HR department.

The Human Resources Department

You've made it through the computer screening and, although your resume is now being read by a human being, you are still being harshly judged. HR usually focuses on the skills, experience, and education of the candidate and how well it matches the job description. Yep – that means we need to have those keywords included once again, but now there is a bit better understanding of what they mean.

Keep this in mind: HR doesn't actually hire anyone. Their job is to CUT candidates more than anything. To do so, they tend to be more literal about candidates needing to match the qualifications while looking for red flags that might make a candidate less desirable.

Don't worry, there is still one saving grace: the hiring managers.

The Hiring Managers

As we explored in Chapter 8: Track Down the Hiring Managers, we know that most hiring managers are just as frustrated with HR as the candidates. They know what they really need in terms of talent, ability, relevant experience, and culture fit. However, those aren't the standards that HR uses to judge the candidates.

What managers really want to know is:

• Who are you and how well will you fit into our company culture?

• What results have you achieved in the past?

• Are you passionate about this line of work?

- Bonus: How does all of this apply to their needs – especially if you are transitioning from a different industry?

Since hiring managers don't care about the keywords as much, it is possible to make a simpler, "networking resume" that is more stylish than the counterparts that need to survive HR's screening processes.

At the Personal Touch Career Services, we have seen many job seekers successfully gain jobs where they weren't the "perfect fit" based on the job description. However, because they were able to convey their overall abilities and passion for the work to the hiring managers, they overcame HR's rigid guidelines and landed in jobs they love.

Outside Recruiters or "Headhunters"

Let's not forget the placement agencies or outside recruiters. In this case, they don't care as much about the keywords, except for some initial screening or hunting up the resumes from employment websites or LinkedIn. Instead, they want to see if they can sell you to a company.

That's right: you are meat.

This is one of the reasons why some recruiters will ask you to revise your resume a certain way to highlight different skills, experience, or achievements. It is to match a *specific* role or company. Those suggestions may not work for different companies or even different opportunities presented by the same recruiter.

While making changes for these recruiters, just keep in mind that they neither care about nor use the same screening processes as HR does. Typically, you would not incorporate those strategies for any resume that you submit directly to an employer.

What About Cover Letters?

According to a survey of Denver-area HR professionals that the Personal Touch Career Services conducted in 2017, only 50% of corporate recruiters felt that a well-written cover letter can help a candidate's chances in getting through the screening process. 10% used them as a screening tool, meaning that anyone who did not submit a cover letter was screened out. The remaining 40% didn't care, and in fact, often didn't even allow for a way to submit them with the application.

So, why suffer writing a personalized cover letter?

Because the real audience is not the HR department.

Those letters are written for the **HIRING MANAGERS**. This makes cover letters the perfect avenue to show off how much you know about the company and how you can really help them achieve their goals.

Tweaking Made Easy: Deciphering the Job Description

Most job descriptions hold the keys to tweaking the resume within it. The trick is understanding what part of the job description relates to what part of the resume.

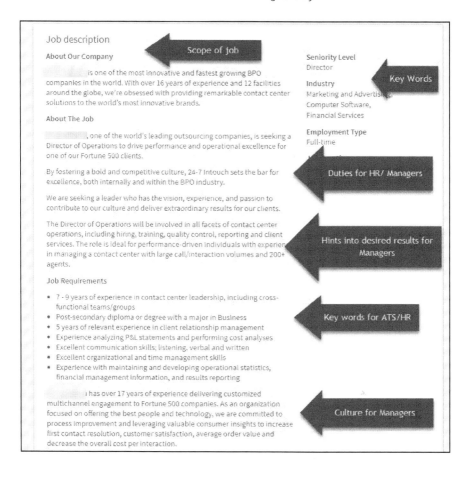

Here's the secret formula:

- Company Descriptions shows the scope and culture of the job.

- Duties or Responsibilities need to relate to your Work Experience's bullet points for HR and managers to see the relevance.

- The Duties will give hints into the desired results and achievements that managers want to see.

- The Requirements or Qualifications hold most of the screening keywords for the ATS and HR.

- Any additional Company Information relates to the company culture.

Tweaked resume follows...

Frank N. Stein

5 Lois Lane | Anytown, USA | 555- 962-4601 | fakeemail@gmail.com
https://www.linkedin.com/in/fake

DIRECTOR OF OPERATIONS

Results-oriented and knowledgeable Executive Project Manager and Ta~~ck~~ aerospace industry. Expertly engages in customer service, global interaction an~~d~~ ding and leadership capabilities. Passionate about analyzing a specific tasking/proj~~e~~ Provides exemplary skills in building new business relationships and strengthening/incre~~a~~ current accounts. Delivers outstanding

Summary: Personality and Passion

> **Offers strong abilities within government contracts,** consistently collaborating with international clients and teams to effectively achieve established initiatives.

> **Consistently achieves organizational goals** through ~~o~~ ng knowledge within the aerospace/aviation industry.

> **Possesses solid business acumen and leadership,** deliveri~~ng~~ nd business partners.

Top Achievements for This Job

PROVEN PROFIT-BUILDING CAPABILITIES

- Business Development
- Project Management
- Aerospace Financial Management

- Team Leadership / Training
- Customer Service
- International Collaboration

Skills: Keywords for ATS/HR

PROFESSIONAL CAREER HISTORY

TCGC., Anytown, USA   2005 – Present
Positons of Increasing Responsibility
Assistant Vice President (2014 - Present)
Currently manage four US government contracts valued at $5.5M. Provide resource allocation strategies for all contracts. Construct consulting strategies for the follow-on fiscal years, and establish consulting business development plans in collaboration with the director of business development. Prepare and deliver technical briefings.
  ✓ Designed a reorganizational consulting structure for heightened efficiency.

Project Manager (2009 - 2014)
Directed the organization's largest government consulting agre~~e~~ ~~se~~parate initiatives within the contract scope. Engaged in complex contra~~ct~~ acquire additional revenue from the US government. Provided monthly deli~~v~~ nce of a diverse and cross-functional team consisting of subject matter experts, g~~overn~~ment engineers, OEMs and US Navy aviators.
  ✓ Provided foreign military groups located in Switzerland, Kuwait, Malaysia, Australia, Finland and Spain with derivative products.
  ✓ Increased corporate revenue by 24% during the past two years.
  ✓ Developed a cross-functional consulting organizational structure, increasing proficiency and communication during a corporate reorganization

Experience: Relevant Duties

PRODUCT LEAD (2005- 2009)
Served as the product lead challenged with developing and creating content for 72 chapters in the documentation. Led a team comprised of 20 expert weapon system engineers and subject matter experts.
  ✓ Managed a $2.9M yearly budget.
  ✓ Served as the senior analyst, expertly providing liaison service~~s~~
  ✓ Appointed as the subject matter expert and voting member for the ~~i~~ncorporating 48 interim clearances into four new software upgrades.

Specific Achievements

EDUCATION AND PROFESSIONAL DEVELOPMENT

Bachelor of Science (B.S.) - Civil Engineering, Big University, CO (2004)

Certifications: Project Management Professional (PMP) (PMI)

Education

When updating a resume to match a specific job, I will frequently print off the job description. As I add or find each element within the resume, I mark it off on the job description. Similarly, if there are items that don't relate to this specific position, they can be removed.

What's great about this exercise is that it can be done very quickly. Ideally, it should take no more than 30 to 90 minutes to tweak out any resume to fit the specific job. If it is taking you longer than this, then your core document was not targeted correctly in the first place. In that case, it may be necessary to do a deep keyword analysis that involves several job descriptions for the same type of job. [Wondering how to do that? Review my chapter on the Key Element Detector in *"How to Get a Job Without Going Crazy (2nd Ed.)."*]

A Note About Scope and Culture

You may have noticed that scope of the job and company culture matter a lot to the managers and the HR department. This is because they want that good match with a candidate, and aligning culture is the current "sexy" way to achieve that goal.

When customizing your resume, find ways to reference the same level the company operates on. In our sample job, the employer noted that they were an international, Fortune 500 company. To make the right impression on a manager, you need to show how you _understand_ that level of business. Just being the Director of Operations for a mid-sized regional manufacturer may not cut it.

However, don't lose hope. Doing things like taking additional professional development courses, expanding your network to larger companies, and showcasing achievements can be ways to open doors and start a conversation. Similarly, this would be an ideal target for setting up an informational interview. After all, those hiring managers didn't start at the top and learning from their example is a great way to gain a foothold.

Chapter 12: Interviewing Practices to Know Before You Go

IT'S NO SECRET: FEW PEOPLE ENJOY INTERVIEWING. That goes double for hiring managers. On both sides of the table, interviews can be awkward, time-consuming, and non-productive. Candidates are nervous and strained. Or worse, they spout what they think the hiring manager wants to hear. Hiring managers can be bored, distracted or even nervous themselves. Frequently, interviewers make judgments on the spot and it can be hard to change that first impression.

Listening to the advice of professional job search advisors can drive you crazy. Some of the clichés don't even make sense, even as they are repeated in the job search community – does "turn your weakness into a strength" sound familiar? Then there are the "rules," which can be overwhelming: don't talk too much, don't say too little, don't wear black, don't talk about your personal life, be sure to mention something about what you enjoy doing outside of work, and so on. It can be difficult to concentrate on the actual interview if you try to play by these rules.

Be Yourself, Be Honest – but Beware

I do not believe in putting up a "front" or a performance in an interview. It is more important to be yourself. Instead of forcing yourself to be something you're not, capitalize on what you have to offer. Not only that, when you try to say what you think the interviewer wants to hear, you won't be able to tell if this job is actually a good fit for you. Modern interviewing is all about making sure that this new employment relationship will be a best match for everyone involved: you, the company itself, and especially your potential boss and coworkers.

You don't need to be an extrovert to ace an interview. Plenty of introverted, nervous, and shy people are hired every day.

A clear example of this is the perceived bias in American-style interviewing for people who are more extroverted. In theory, one would think that the candidates who are most likely to win a job are those who are outgoing, personable, congenial, and relaxed when meeting new people. However, this myth doesn't fit all situations. It really depends on the company culture and all about being yourself. I have seen a lot of introverted or nervous people do worse in an interview because they are trying to operate outside of their comfort zone. Instead of acknowledging their discomfort, they push themselves to be outgoing, which looks fake and forced to an interviewer. On the flip side, as a recruiter, I have been just as easily impressed with someone who is reserved but still confident in their abilities. It comes down to preparation, not personality.

Be yourself, but plan ahead and practice, practice, practice – especially crucial moments of the interview itself, such as your introduction, your closing, and the typical tough questions you know you will face. By being yourself, you can be confident that the job will be an excellent match for your personality, skills, experience, and future ambitions. And yes, this is what the company is seeking as well: they are just as invested in finding a good match for their culture – that is, if they are a quality employer and not just someone who is hoping to find a warm body to throw into the job.

Next, you want to be honest during the interview. It is okay for you to talk about your professional passions, your goals, and your expectations. When describing your skills, don't overinflate your abilities but don't be afraid to brag a bit about your strengths. Of course, always follow up these strong statements with solid examples or situations that directly relate to the job.

Honesty also extends to the difficult situations, such as being let go from a job. In modern interviewing, it is very common to be asked questions that are inherently negative, such as, "Tell us about a time that you failed." In any negative situation, you do need to answer honestly, but what is most important is what you learned or how you would have treated it differently. I will give you a lot of opportunities to practice questions like this in Appendix III: Practice Interview Questions.

Finally, you need to beware. Don't let your brains fall on the floor. This is a competitive situation, and you do want to put your best foot forward.

"Beware" also means "be aware." Be aware of the interviewer, including body language, voice, and what is not being said. If you only concentrate on your own performance, you miss the subtle clues that say tons about a working environment.

What Interviewers Really Want To Know

At every one of the interview phases, the employers want to know four basic questions:

1. Can you do the job?

This is all about the technical skills (smart keywords) – do you have the ability to carry out the duties of the job? Depending on the demands of the position, this can get very detailed. Be prepared to answer with actual examples from your experience.

2. Will you fit into our company culture?

These questions relate to how your personality and style will mesh with their corporate culture. Depending on the company or situation, this could be more or less important. Don't be fooled – even if they never ask questions down this path, they are making personal judgments based on your appearance, your actions, and your reactions.

3.   Do you have any issues?

While similar to the culture questions, what interviewers really want to know is how well you work with others. They could be fishing for your attitude about past employers. Are you blaming the company or former boss for any of your negative outcomes? Is your frustration shining through? What are your concerns in a workplace? Why do you have discrepancies in your work history?

4.   Can I get you at the right price?

Some things are about the bottom line. However, just because salary will definitely be a factor, that does not mean that you can't negotiate for the best possible situation for yourself.

Employers' Goals at Each Stage of the Interview Process

Depending on the interview stage, the questions will be emphasized differently.

Every phase of the employment cycle addresses specific objectives for the employers. Creating the job description identifies their needs. Screening tools are designed to quickly reveal the top applicants. Similarly, each phase of interviewing process hopes to reveal different aspects about the candidates.

Understanding the employer's goals puts some control back in your hands as well as making sure you are on their unstated agenda. For example, if you are undergoing a screening telephone interview, you don't need to go into deep explanations of highly technical applications, such as a very skilled software developer trying to explain the full Agile software development lifecycle to an entry-level HR person who is just trying to screen her on the salary range. On the other hand, that same candidate could give very detailed answers during her interview with the hiring manager, because that person will actually understand all of the technical jargon. When you are meeting the rest of the team, try to relax, as this is really a culture match test to see if you might be the "right fit" for their department

Stage	Conducted by...	Goal	How to Handle
Phone Interview	Lower level HR person	Screening on basics	• Schedule time, don't wing it • Have copy of job description • Don't gush - stick to facts
First Interview	HR department	Skills Fit Professionalism	• Dress for success • Bring copies of resume • Be prepared to answer technical questions • Have intelligent questions
Second Interview	Managers	Ability assessment Culture fit Negotiation feelers	• Tailor presentation to the person • Research them online beforehand • Higher level technical questions • Be personable
Subsequent interviews	Other managers, team members	Culture	• Be yourself, but cautious • Don't contradict earlier answers or images
Procedure Points	HR department	Checking references Legal requirements	• Be helpful
Job Offer	HR or Manager	Get you at the best price	• Be ready to negotiate

The phone interview: Technical abilities and price range

Phone interviews concern the "can you do the job" and "are you the right price" issues. A phone interview is first and foremost a screening tool. Lower-level employees usually conduct phone interviews and gauge your answers against the given qualifications. Screeners could also look for the basic technical proficiency required for the job. Their goal is to bring you in or cut you, a judgment made within 15 minutes or less.

You should always expect phone interview question like these:

1. Are you still interested?

Hopefully, the screener will give you some more information about the job, or at least remind you of the open position. With multiple candidates, verifying availability is a priority for the employer. They don't want to waste time chasing uninterested candidates.

1. Verification of your skill set

You will be asked about the skills listed on your resume as they relate to the posted job description. In addition to confirming the information, try to include an example, while still keeping the answer quick and to the point.

2. Brief summary of why you're looking

Make sure you know how to answer this in a concise way, without pussy-footing around or bemoaning your situation. Develop a simple, clear answer for this question ahead of time. It is acceptable to mention you were laid off, by the way. If you were let go for other reasons, be sure to have a rehearsed answer. Refrain from disclosing too many details to keep your own tone positive.

3. What salary are you looking for?

If possible, speak only in terms of salary range. Naming your range is acceptable, but pinning down a specific number at this point is not a good idea. If you aren't comfortable with stating a number first, ask the interviewer what *their* salary range is. You don't want to waste time chasing something below your goals.

One variation on the salary question is when they ask what you were making in your last job. This may seem unfair, especially if your salary expectations have changed drastically (either up or down). When answering, you can point out that your circumstances have changed. Unfortunately, because you are dealing with an entry-level person at this point, they may push back harder for a firm answer. They don't have the authority or the knowledge to do otherwise.

The first interview: In-depth technical skills and first impressions

Your first in-person interview involves information gathering on both sides of the table. Employers will tell you more about the company and the expectations for the job. You will be sharing your experience and abilities. Conversation will turn to why you are interested in their job. You should project a desire to learn more about the opportunity.

At this point, you may encounter another screening, either from HR or from the hiring manager's department. Either way, expect technical questions that will be much more challenging. Brush up on those skills. Before the interview, write down some real-world examples to help you remember. Technical questions often comprise the majority of the first interview.

One of the first questions will be, "How much do you know about our company?" Don't miss this critical step! Failing to look up the company and compile your knowledge says, "I don't care about your company or your job." Even a simple five-minute perusal of their website can remind you about what draws you to the company. Develop your own questions – insightful, relevant and interesting questions shows your intelligence. Remember, you are trying to be relevant to the employer's needs. You must be familiar with who they are and what they do.

You will be judged by the way you look; that's human nature. In fact, visual appearance is one of the strongest factors in making a positive first impression. Wearing a suit may not be mandatory for employees, but you may want to strongly consider it for the very first job interview. Even in a traditionally casual industry, dress up for an interview. This conveys respect for the interviewer and your interest in the job. If the office is more casual, you can dress down some for the second interview.

The only exception to the suit rule is if the company tells you what to wear. One major company would tell applicants to come to the interview wearing shorts. Anybody who didn't follow those specific instructions was cut.

Don't wear heavy fragrances (both men and women). Smells can turn negative very quickly in a closed office, and you never know who will be allergic to what. Sparkly or loud jewelry can be just as annoying.

Dress up your resume as well. Bring a printed copy with you, on a good resume stock. 24 lb. paper works well, however, avoid card stock (60 lb. and higher). It gives people nasty paper cuts. Bring several copies, in case others sit in on the interview. Always have a copy for yourself.

The second interview: Personality and culture

Congratulations – you are probably meeting the hiring manager at this point. This could be right after you finish the first interview, or they could bring you in a second time. Personality and culture are the keys here. You passed the technical skills assessment, which may have included a formal test. The manager will ask you about those skills again; however, the focus will shift because the manager really does understand what she needs out of the employee. In many cases, HR's understanding of the position may be different from what the actual position is. Pay close attention to what the hiring manager is saying about the job to root out any misinterpretation on HR's part.

Subsequent interviews: The right fit

Most hiring decisions are made during the subsequent interviews, including any "informal" tours of the facility or opportunities to meet team members. If you're working with a management team to land a senior-level position, expect to come in a few more times to make sure you fit with everyone else. Third interviews are all about the corporate culture. Count yourself lucky if you get a chance to check out the team before making your decision.

Talking about money...

One of the biggest shifts in modern interviewing is the salary issue. While the old-school rules were to never discuss money or benefits until the offer was pending, everything changed during the Great Recession of 2008. It became crucial for employers to know what salary the job seekers wanted, especially since they were constantly dealing with a deluge of candidates for every single job opening. If someone wasn't within their salary range, HR didn't want to waste the time for multiple interviews just to discover that their top choice was way out of their price range. While HR isn't as overwhelmed by candidates today, the procedure of screening based on salary is ingrained as standard operations for most employers.

In the modern job search, companies frequently ask the candidate's salary requirements during the early interviews, sometimes even during the phone interview. The good news is that since HR brings up these topics early in the process, it is acceptable for candidates to ask about the company's target salary range even if HR doesn't broach the subject. However, by the time you reach the manager, your focus should be about the job and not your personal gains.

1. <u>Know your worth.</u>

Even before you apply for a job, you need to do your research into what are the current market rates for your target job. Thanks to websites like Glassdoor.com and Salary.com, it is easier than ever to figure out comparable salaries, both within a specific employer and a targeted geographic area. Additional resources are the Bureau of Labor Statistics (www.bls.gov) and state-specific employment data, such as the Colorado Labor Market Indicator Gateway (https://www.colmigateway.com). Armed with solid figures about the current state of the market is critical in gaining a fair salary.

2.   Find out their salary range before you state any numbers.

The old interviewing rules stated that you never wanted to talk about salary during the interview process. However, that's not how the game works anymore. This changed because HR now uses salary requirements as a screening factor. For example, it is now a common practice for HR to gain a candidate's salary requirements during the phone interview. Look out – it's a trap! Don't ever give out your salary requirement without discovering their salary range first.

So, how does one find out the company's salary range? During the phone interview or early interviews with the HR department, ask them. This can play out two different ways. Either HR asks you, or you broach the subject.

Scenario 1: HR asks your desired salary

> *HR: What salary are you hoping to get for this job?*

> *CANDIDATE: As we are still discussing the scope of the job, that can be difficult to pin down. Can you give me an idea on what your salary range is?*

> *[AWKWARD SILENCE]*

> *HR: Well, we have budgeted a salary range of $70,000 to $80,000.*

Scenario 2: You ask HR the salary range

> HR: I think this wraps up my questions. Do you have any questions for me?

> Candidates: Yes, I do. I noticed that the salary wasn't posted in the job description. Could you give me an idea of what your salary range is?

> [AWKWARD SILENCE]

> HR: Well, we have budgeted a salary range of $70,000 to $80,000.

The awkward silence is crucial for both scenarios. Practice both situations with others. Similarly, if you can't get them to share their range first, you may have to give yours. In all cases, say your numbers with confidence – nothing cheapens a job offer like a candidate who meekly says, "well, I was hoping for something around $70,000, but I will take $65,000."

3. Avoid sending your salary history if possible.

Sometimes HR wants you to send your salary history. This is another trap! If you give your salary history, you just gave away your negotiation strength. Companies look at salary history to determine a salary offer. HR knows that many people change jobs to increase their salary by as little as 5% to 7%. If the employer knows the details of your past earnings, they may offer less based on your salary history. The only exception to the salary history rule is a professional salesperson, especially in commissioned positions. In that case, salary history is a reflection of success.

If you are in a situation or application that won't let you move forward without entering this information, be sure to state your salary range within your cover letter to let an employer know what your expectations are.

4. Understand the company's negotiation tactics.

The truth is that HR and hiring managers almost always have a second offer in their back pockets. They know that a certain amount of leeway is reasonable, and even expected. But they also know that most job seekers won't make a counter-offer, which translates to a win for their overall budgets.

When getting a job offer, ask for that extra 5% – 15% on the salary. Pressing for more than this can be seen as unreasonable, and those are the offers that will be pulled. I know that nothing annoyed me more, as an HR person, than the salesman who suddenly counter-offered a 30% – or more – jump on the base salary. That just wasted everyone's time.

5. Back up your reasoning for a higher salary with solid evidence.

When you are moving into a new position, sometimes you may need to justify why you are worth all of that extra money. This could be a number of reasons, such as the current market rate. If you have added to your skills, this is another reason. Gaining a new degree, certification, or professional development courses also add to your worth. Don't forget your progressive experience and specific projects or results that you achieved for your past employer as well.

However, one of the best reasons for asking for a higher salary is based on what you can do for the company. If you can prove during the course of the interview process that you can help them save money, make money, or solve problems, this allows them to find more dollars in their budget.

But what if they say "No?"

Even if the company doesn't accept your counter-offer, the world didn't end. Most reasonable employers will be forthright about not being able to increase the offer. Then you can still accept the original terms.

On the other hand, if the company completely rescinds the offer, you probably just dodged a bullet. After all, any company that will yank an offer off the table just because you tried to negotiate tends to be a pretty negative culture. They are trying to take advantage of their employees.

Interview the company: Develop your own questions

You always want to prepare your own questions. Every interviewer will ask, "Do you have any questions?" It is death to answer, "Uh, what are the benefits?" Be prepared and have intelligent questions relating to the company, the job and your own goals.

When developing your questions, consider these categories:

1. Fact-finding

Facts cover everything from daily duties to department organization. It is the mechanics of the job and how you can perform them. Fact-finding covers the subtle layers that your research can't tell you.

Examples: Who manages this position? What are the key responsibilities and duties? Has someone been in this position before? What did they do well? What did you dislike?

2. Opportunity

Find out as much as you can about the job itself. How does it fit with your goals? This could be confirming what you already know from your own research, but it's interesting to hear what the management says by comparison. On another level, these give you a chance to show off your research by asking related questions.

> *Examples: Where do you see the company going in the next few years? I read about ___ industry challenge; how are you handling it? What is your marketing strategy for your new product line?*

3. Competition

Ask about the company's hiring process. Find out where you stand without going off the deep end.

> *Examples: Do you have many more interviews scheduled? When will you be making a final decision?*

4. Uncovering Bad Situations

Want to avoid a control-freak or negative work situations? You had better ask some questions relating to this area. While you can't ask "are you a screaming maniac?" Try these instead:

How is your turnover rate?

If their eyes wander the room while they hesitantly reply, "we had some people who weren't the right fit," look out.

What is the biggest challenge in this job?

Watching their body language tells you more than their words. If the biggest challenge is a control freak boss, the interviewer may hesitate or look away rather than offer a direct answer.

Has this position been open for long?

Difficult jobs are hard to fill and stay open longer. Or, conversely, the job has only been open for a week is a bad sign as well. That means the company is a meat grinder, crushing new employees who need to be replaced immediately.

If you're wary of a bad situation, pay attention to the people in the office. Are people jumping when the boss calls on the phone? Do they look strained and anxious? Can you cut the tension with a knife? Are you separated from the company's employees during the interview process? These are all bad signs – ignore them at your own peril.

Room setup, territory, and body language

As with all human interaction, non-verbal communication is a vital element in interviews. Room arrangement reveals a specific message about the company. A cubicle-world environment with few personal items is not supportive to the employees. A messy office can be signs of overwork; nobody has time to clean things.

When you arrive at the office, take some time to notice your surroundings. Talk to the receptionist. After all, the hiring manager will ask her how you acted in the lobby.

When you are brought back for the interview, check out the room. All companies will consciously or sub-consciously arrange their environment to set a specific mood or control of everyone involved. Furniture setup can indicate the tone of the interview. Some of the most common setups include:

The Distant 1-on-1

If you are meeting with someone in their office, pay attention to the chairs in relation to the desk. If your chair is smaller, lower, or uncomfortable, the interviewer is trying to intimidate you. A classic example of this is the executive in a huge, stately chair while yours is hard and stiff-backed. Just like the animal kingdom, predators may puff themselves up to be more intimidating to the prey. Similarly, if your chair is far away from their desk, the interviewer is keeping you distant to make judgment easier. Angles that are straight-on have a confrontational feel as well.

The Friendly 1-on-1

Not all in-office interviews are about power plays. Chairs placed off to the side of a desk or at 45-degree angle are more casual, inviting, and comfortable. If your chair is placed closer to the desk, this allows you to have some physical separation and "cover" when facing hard questions. Even though you are physically closer, this inviting attitude is designed to make you relax. It's like meeting with a friend, as opposed to being stared down by a senior manager.

Important note: Territory Issues

Anytime you are meeting in someone's office, be aware of invading their territory. Sometimes you can be the problem! Don't place anything on the interviewer's desk without asking permission. Definitely avoid leaning on their desk, as that is like an all-out invasion. Similarly, don't move any of the chairs in the room without asking permission. Remember, all environments are set up either consciously or subconsciously; moving the chairs destroys that setup, which also destroys your ability to analyze the hidden messages about the work environment in general.

The Conference Room Interview

Many times, you won't be meeting people in their office. In this case, some of the rules change. For example, everyone is now in neutral territory, so you don't need to ask permission to rest your notebook or folder on the table. When offered a choice of seats, try to avoid sitting with your back to the door. That way, you can easily acknowledge anyone else who may arrive. Look for ways to create the 45-degree angle, especially if meeting with only one or two people.

The Traditional Panel

Panels, by their very nature, are intimidating. No one likes the idea or mental image of being grilled by a group of key decision makers. However, this doesn't mean that the company chose the panel format to intimidate you. Sometimes, it is a matter of convenience or even regulation. For example, when I worked for the PBS television station in Denver, we always had to have a diverse panel of interviewers to satisfy not only FCC regulations, but also requirements for our federal grants and non-profit status.

Your best clues on if this meant to be intimidating or not comes down to the room setup. Just like the Distant 1-on-1 interview, the further back your chair is from the panel, the more judgmental it is. A small, uncomfortable, hard-backed chair that is three feet away from the panel is definitely designed to increase your stress levels.

The Boardroom Panel

A more modern version of the panel takes place in the boardroom or conference room. In this case, the candidate is seated at the foot of the table, with all of the heavy hitters lining both sides of the table. Of course, the head of the table is reserved for the most senior-ranking member of the panel. These interviews may even require a formal presentation by the candidate, which could include handouts or audio/visual components. These challenging interviews are usually reserved for top management, highly technical roles, and education or training positions.

Crucial tip for panel interviews

No matter how the room is set up, if you are interviewing with more than one person, be sure to address them all equally. Engage in eye contact with everyone in the room and make them feel that you are speaking to them personally. Don't worry if someone is silent and reserved. Even if he never asks a question, he was included on the panel for a reason.

Body Language

Body language says a lot. Most people tend to lean forward if they are interested in the person they meet. If they use hand gestures, watch where the direction is aimed. If their hands move towards you, it is meant to be engaging. However, if they are pulling their hands inward, they are withdrawing from the conversation. The worst case would be someone who has their arms crossed over their chest. That is practically radiating a closed mind (unless they are very cold!) If their hands are behind their head, they are mentally out to lunch or completely self-absorbed.

Notice the position of their hands. Do they cover their mouth, or are their hands under their chin? While some people will cover parts of their face when lying or trying to hide something, it means something different if you are meeting with an introvert. In that case, these movements convey inward reflection. It this gives them physical distance to consider things.

Body Language Suggestions for You

Use a firm, normal handshake. Maintain eye contact and remember to blink. Sit comfortably in the chair, but not all the way back. You should be more forward, showing your interest in what the interviewer is saying. You want to keep the contact open. If you talk with your hands, don't let them fly all over the place. In that case, try to restrain more by keep your hands in your lap. What you think are minimal movements tend to be exaggerated in stressful situations.

If you're introverted by nature, that is perfectly okay. A big myth in job searching is that only outgoing, gregarious people do well in interviews, and therefore they are the ones getting hired. Truth is, being comfortable with yourself conveys a lot more than being overly bold. Don't chastise yourself. Find a way to make your nature work for you. For example, taking time to answer questions shows thoughtfulness, not weakness.

What not to do:

- Don't chew gum or anything else.

- Don't lose your sense of humor.

- Don't smoke beforehand.

- Make sure you say each interviewer's name at least once.

- While chemistry is important in an interview, it is not the only factor. If rapport or a genuine connection is not there, don't give up – it may not be as bad as you think.

Handling Different Interviewer Styles

Employers try all kinds of different tactics for interviews. Some will subject you to a veritable stress test, just to see how you react. Or they may act friendly, setting you at ease so that you reveal more than originally intended.

However, not every interviewer is a polished interview expert. The manager may be just as nervous as you. In any case, anticipating these various styles and knowing how to deal with them can help you ace even the worst interview situation.

Friendly and Personable

Don't be fooled! By being open and nice, the interviewer is putting you at ease, getting you to lower your guard. In truth, he is evaluating everything you say. Candidates will reveal more in a relaxed atmosphere. Ever come out of an interview convinced you're hired because you "really connected" – only to be shocked when you didn't get the job? You were taken in by the Friendly Style.

Survival Tactic:

Don't get too comfortable. Stay on your toes and keep your goals in mind.

Nervous and Uncomfortable

This is not an act! Not all hiring managers are smooth and polished. The interview process can intimidate them as well. If he tends to ramble on about the job and forget to ask questions, he's stumbling through it. Likewise, his questions may be very terse and limited. Body language is a clear give-away here. Nervous interviewers make less eye contact, may pore over the resume, and may even hunch in their chairs. It is possible to engage them, but don't overpower.

Survival Tactic:

Take the lead. Offer to tell him about your experience and skills. Be proactive with your questions. Ask him what he did or didn't like about the last person in the job. Be sure to ask what his expectations are going forward.

The Skeptic

Here's the grumpy interviewer. Everything about his manner is re-served and distant. He doesn't seem to believe anything you're saying. Why? There are a couple of reasons for this attitude. First, somebody let him down before. Whether it was the person they just let go or a bad employee from a year ago, he does not want to make the same mistake twice. As a result, he is hard to deal with in the interview. Second, he may be expecting you to sell yourself. By limiting the non-verbal communication, he hopes that you will not react to subtle clues as to what he's looking for. It's a way to derail candidates from saying what she wants to hear.

Survival Tactic:
Drop the touchy-feely answers and use solid examples of your accomplishments. Maintain your good humor and self-confidence. Remember, he's trying to rattle you by acting cold.

The Bored and the Boring

This interviewer may seem completely withdrawn. He could look lethargic, listless, or just plain bored. You could be his fourth interview of the day or he just had a heavy lunch. Everything says he's just not into you (yawn.) Be careful, though; don't mistake an introvert for boredom.

Survival Tactic:

Be concise and get to the point. Show your own enthusiasm for the job by revving up your energy level. Ask him about himself. People like to talk about themselves, and this could bring him into your conversation

.

The Introvert

The Introvert appears reserved and distant, but not to the degree of the Skeptic. He tends to sit back in his chair during an interview – not because he isn't engaged, but because he is taking everything in. Introverts tend to cover their mouths when they are thinking. Another clear indication is when he looks away to think about something you just said. This is a process of internalization, especially if the eyes shift up. On the whole, Introverts are quiet, calm, observant, and very, very sharp.

Survival Tactic:

Unlike the Bored interviewer, showing too much enthusiasm can overwhelm the Introvert. Overloading him can be taken almost as a threat and is certainly a major culture clash. Instead, match the pacing and body language of the interviewer to build nonverbal rapport.

By The Book

This is a process-driven person. He has his list of questions and he's sticking to them no matter what. Often times, he tries to write down your answers during the interview. So what is up with that? His position in the company can give a clue as to his motive. For example, if he's from the HR department or someone's assistant, he's running you through the screening process. A manager who uses this tactic is a process-driven person, methodical in everything he does. Or she might be using her prepared questions to hide his own introverted nature.

Survival Tactic:

Let him have his process. Answer questions fully, but give him time to write his answers. It is actually a big pet peeve if you keep talking while he's writing. After all, he can't stop writing until you stop answering the question! This is an efficient person who expects people to get to the point. Stay on his agenda and follow his methodology.

Surreal

Not too long ago, an interviewing fad hit the internet: throw bizarre questions at candidates to see how they think. "How many quarters does it take to reach the top of the Empire State Building?" "If you lined up hamsters nose to tail, how many would it take to reach the moon?" "How would you sort a bucket of golf balls?" All this goofiness was supposed to give insight into your problem-solving skills. In practice, it's just weird and few managers do this anymore. On the other hand, progressive companies like Google use logic tests to weed out candidates. In that case, you DO need the right answer to move forward in the process.

Survival Tactic:

Think before you answer. The actual answer doesn't matter. These questions give insight into your thinking process, personality, and flexibility.

Highly Technical

If you are going after a very technical job, be prepared for this type of interviewer. You may encounter very specific and detailed questions to test your knowledge. Timed and graded skills tests could be part of the assessment.

One engineer I know interviews all the new PhD candidates for a Research & Design company. He grilled them on specific formulas and principles for over an hour. For example, if an applicant didn't know the exact definition and mathematical equation for entropy, he would get marked down – and saw the marks being made on his resume. (In physics, entropy is a thermodynamic quantity representing the unavailability of a system's thermal energy for conversion into mechanical work, often interpreted as the degree of disorder or randomness in the system. Just in case you didn't know.) Candidates left the office feeling like they just took the worst college exam of their lives and failed it. Certainly, it was the most grueling interview they would ever encounter. However, people did get hired; just because a test is tough doesn't mean you lost the opportunity.

Under tough conditions like this, even the best of candidates may only score a 50%. In fact, I know of several IT leaders who set up the test to be nearly impossible to score even 60% of the answers right. Not only are they testing the job seekers' knowledge, they want to see how they stand up to stress.

Survival Tactic:

Think before you answer. If you're struggling with an answer, don't let it rattle you too badly. Prepare for this interview: study up on key points, skills, or processes necessary for your job.

Deliberately Confrontational

For some reason, top executives tend to favor this type of interview style because they think they are an "excellent judge of character." Everything about this interviewer's attitude screams "I'm gonna get ya!" He is dismissive, he cuts you off, and he drills into your answers with an air of scorn. Why? He wants to see how you act under pressure. Don't worry; he may not be like this in the workplace. Oftentimes, he will be a completely different person on the second interview. His philosophy is to see you sweat in the interview; that way, he knows you can handle the job. However, if you face this type of person, try to network with some of the current or past employees afterwards to see if this attitude carries over into the regular workday.

Survival tactic:

Don't forget to breathe! Get grounded and stay focused. Don't give in to the stress or get upset. It will be over soon!

Multiple person interviews

In some cases, you will interview with more than one person. Panel interviews make the most of everyone's time. You will normally be notified about a panel interview ahead of time. If not, don't be scared. Just roll with the punches. Part of the test is seeing how you adapt to unexpected situations.

Panels can be combinations of several interview styles, with each person taking a different role. After the interview, the panel members compare notes, sharing their impressions from different points of view.

Good Cop / Bad Cop

Yes, it's cheesy as hell, but some people watch too much TV. It's really a combination of a Friendly-style interviewer with the Confrontational type.

Survival Tactic:

Remember, this set-up is an act. Deal with each interviewer in a consistent manner. They are looking for the conflicting answers.

Redirection

If two people are in the room, who is the boss? Are you sure? They may even throw conflicting body language. One could be checking his email while the other is a very engaging conversationalist. Be sure to address *both*. This is a power play on their part, seeing if you can keep it straight.

Survival Tactic:

Stay focused on the principal, or the one with the authority. If you aren't sure who it is, address both equally, even if one is ignoring you. He is there for a reason. It is acceptable to ask questions about who your direct supervisor would be.

Panel Interviews

Some companies use panel interviews as a matter of policy. Only one person may ask the questions, or they may take turns. You could easily run into all the individual interviewer styles. However, the panel itself is not designed to "get you." It is ultimately a time saver for the company, allowing for multiple opinions of all the candidates in one meeting.

Survival Tactic:

Address your answers to everyone. Make eye contact at least twice with every member. Don't forget to breathe and keep your sense of humor.

Final Thoughts on Interviewer Styles

No matter how many interviewer styles you encounter, try to keep your own cool. Notice your own personal style of interviewing: are you nervous? Are you friendlier? Are you withdrawn? Try practicing with others to see where your own abilities fall. From there, you can learn to adapt to any interview situation.

Chapter 13: Strategies to Ace the Interview

FOR MOST PEOPLE, the biggest concern with interviewing is how to answer the tough questions – or, for some, answering any of the questions! Some questions have certainly become predictable over the decades, such as, "What is your greatest weakness?" However, modern interviewing goes way beyond these stereotypical questions, forcing candidates to talk about negative situations honestly without falling for the temptation to badmouth their former employers or coworkers.

Fear not, gentle reader. I will give you effective solutions for all these scenarios, from the predictable standard questions to the complex demands of behavioral interviewing. Remember, even as you prepare your answers, you still want to hold fast to the three tenets of interviewing: Be yourself, be honest, and beware.

Different Types of Questions

Depending on how a question is phrased, the interviewer may be looking for a simple answer, a complex description of a process, or a specific story from the past. If you pay attention to HOW the question is presented, you can develop answers that relate to what the interviewer really wants to know. This is why listening is one of the most important things you can do during the interview.

Here's a clear example of a case where not listening to the interviewer cost an applicant the job. I was hiring a new assistant for my company, and I was really excited to speak with a certain candidate. He had an interesting background and his resume looked like he might be able to grow into other roles for our organization. However, when I conducted the phone interview, he had at least one story and sometimes two for every single question I asked. At the end of 30 minutes, I only got through one-third of my questions. I did not have extra time to try to get the remaining questions squeezed in, as I had other appointments. Because I never completed the screening interview, there was no way that I could accurately judge if he would fit into our company. Not to mention the unspoken fear that he would bring these time-sucking tendencies into our regular work day. As a result, he never earned the opportunity to prove me wrong at an in-person interview. I had to move on.

See how important it is to be on the employer's agenda?

Regardless of the type of interview – telephone, virtual, or in-person – there are five basic types of questions:

1. Direct

Direct questions just need a simple answer. Often used as screening tools, you would rarely need to go into too much depth or add a story to your answer.

> *Examples: What is your proficiency level with Microsoft Excel? How many years of experience do you have with B2B sales?*

2. Open-Ended

In this case, the interviewer is expecting you to fill in the details on a process or give your opinion on an issue. Typically speaking, your answer would be more in-depth than the direct question, because you do need to explain all the steps involved or defend your position.

> *Examples: How would you set up a pivot table in Microsoft Excel? What is your favorite sales technique when giving a technical presentation to key decision makers? In your opinion, how do you think the new regulation in our industry will impact manufacturing?*

3. Situational

Formally known as behavioral interviewing, these questions require you to think of a specific incident from your past. Many times, the questions start with statements like: "Tell me about a time when..." or "Describe a situation..." While we will get more in-depth with behavioral interviewing, just keep in mind that it is critical to think of a real-world situation that directly relates to their question. Within your answer you need to address four key components: setting up the situation itself, a description of your task or role, the specific actions you took, and the final result. This forms the foundation for a STAR answer (Situation, Task, Action, Result.)

> *Examples: Tell me about a time when you gave excellent customer service. Describe a time when you found a better way to accomplish a typical task at work – how did you get your boss to accept and implement the new procedures? Tell me about a time when you failed to meet your goals.*

4. Hypothetical or Problem-Solving

Unlike the situational questions, you are not required to think of a specific story; however, you CAN use one if it is appropriate. The goal here is to reveal how your personality traits, experience, skills, or education will be used to solve potential issues.

> *Examples: What would you do to calm down an upset customer? If you only had one hour to prepare a new presentation, what would you do first? If there was one thing you could change at your current job, what would it be?*

Many times, job seekers struggle with identifying a specific situation in a behavioral-based interview. Instead, they give a hypothetical answer based on what they would do. Avoid this at all costs! Interviewers hate it when a candidate fails to come up with a real-world situation when it was clearly requested. If you legitimately don't have a story that relates to their question, be sure to acknowledge that:

Interviewer: "Tell me about a time you had to fire an under-performing employee."

Candidate: "While I never had to fire someone in my past roles, here is how I would handle that situation..."

As you can see, clearly defining your experience followed by the hypothetical answer is always better than immediately jumping into the theory.

5. Reflective

The final type of question is known as the reflective, as it "reflects back" into one of your previous answers or something on your resume. Usually, only trained interviewers will use this technique, as it isn't a common conversational pattern.

Examples: You mentioned that you are an expert in all the Office 365 programs; which one do you use the most in your daily work? I noticed that you had a gap in your work history a couple of years ago – can you tell me why? You stated that you were laid off from your last job – how many other people were laid off at the same time?

Dealing with Common Interview Questions

Now that you understand more about the basic types of questions, let's develop strategies for some of the most common specific questions you will get in the interview.

For each one of these interview questions, brainstorm at least three answers for each of these questions. Don't limit any answer; in fact, include at least one goofy answer – such as your greatest weakness is chocolate or shopping for shoes. Some of the answers that surface may be brutally honest, like your greatest weakness is how you handle conflict or stress. Whatever comes to mind just let it flow from your brain to your pen.

If you do enough writing, the honest and true answer will become apparent.

THEN you get to apply your "beware" filter. While some answers may be 100% true, it may not be the best answer in an interview situation. For example, you would never say "my greatest weakness is that I am late to everything." Nobody wants to hire someone who is chronically late! Just file that one away as something that you need to work on...

The best answers are the ones that are believable in addition to being honest. Years ago, while I was developing these interview techniques, I did a lot of soul-searching to find my weaknesses. What came out on top was the fact that I don't self-promote in work situations. I am not the kind of person who toots her own horn to the boss, letting her know all the wonderful extras that I did for the company every day. My co-workers knew, because I would constantly ask if I could help them out. However, the boss never saw that, and I actually got marked down on a performance review because she didn't know all the extra work I took on. So, for me, self-promotion was a real problem. But here's the rub: that answer doesn't work in an interview situation. After spending 30 minutes talking about how great I was, nobody believed that I didn't self-promote! While it was a brilliant and real answer, it was completely unbelievable.

Don't be satisfied with the first answer. Dig deep to get more options, just in case your first instincts need to be adjusted.

"So, tell us a bit about yourself!"

What is the first question at almost every interview? "Tell us about yourself!"

Believe it or not, a shocking number of candidates don't know how to answer this question. Since this is your first impression, there is a lot riding on this, spanning far beyond just what you say. In fact, it is your most important answer in the entire interview.

What to avoid:
1. Don't go on too long or too short.

The last thing an interviewer wants is a five-minute speech. Your personal introduction should not be more than 30 to 60 seconds long. Hitting this mark saves you from rambling or from saying too little.

2. Don't repeat your resume UNLESS...

... they SPECIFICALLY say, "Walk me through your resume." Trust me, it is extremely boring to the interviewer when someone starts off with their college degree and then talks about every single job they held over the past 15 years. You are going to spend the next 30 to 60 minutes talking about your work history in depth. Don't drown them with details in the first moments of the interview.

3. Don't throw it back to them.

Interviewers especially hate it when a candidate says, "Uh, what would you like to know?" This not only comes across as unprepared, it screams a lack of confidence. Have a prepared introduction.

4. Don't bring family into it.

Or any other "protected" status either, such as health, nationality, race, religion, or even sexual orientation. I have seen plenty of candidates tell me private information that I can't legally ask them, such as telling me that they are married with three kids in elementary school. Yikes! While you want to match the company's culture, being too personal drives the focus away from your abilities and into that protected life. Plus, you don't know how they are going to take it. I worked for one boss who was strongly prejudiced against hiring single mothers because, and I quote, "They have to take too much time off to deal with kid issues." While that is TOTALLY illegal, if a candidate started talking about her children in the interview, there is no possible way for the boss to un-learn it when making her hiring decision.

EXCEPTION: now, this must be handled delicately, but there are a lot of people who are re-entering the workforce after taking a break to raise their children or care for ailing parents. Be expected to address the issue of your recent employment gap; however, DON'T make it the very first thing you state in your introduction.

Best Practices:

1. <u>Engage all the interviewer's learning styles in the first minute: Visual, auditory, and kinesthetic</u>

A big trick to being remembered and liked is to activate these three main learning styles. For example, when you first shake hands, state your name. Now, I know what you're thinking: "They already know my name. It's on my resume!"

People commonly forget names. Your interviewer may be meeting 10 or even 15 different people for this job. Saying your full name activates the auditory learners and helps them associate it with your face and your resume.

For visual learners, everything about your personal presence matters. From the way you are dressed to how you sit in the chair, you want to appear confident, composed, and eager to learn more about the job.

Reaching kinesthetic learners, or those who learn by doing or by experiencing new things, can be challenging if you don't know the tricks. Essentially, you want to make them engage with your physically. While a firm handshake is a start, this is the REAL reason you bring copies of your resume to the interview. This way, you can physically hand it to the interviewer. Similarly, bring business cards or a printed list of your references to leave behind. (Of course, make sure their formats match your resume to engage visual learners at the same time.)

2. <u>Write out and practice your introduction.</u>

It is not enough to just write the introduction. Practice it until it is *almost* memorized. This way, you won't have "ums' and "uhs" creeping into it, but it will still sound natural. Not only that, knowing how you will start your interview will reduce your own nervousness. It keeps you focused, comfortable, and confident.

Creating Your Job-Specific Elevator Speech Introduction

In the business world, the concept of an elevator speech has survived for decades. The name "elevator speech" derives from the concept of how you would entice a stranger to take your business card during a 30-second elevator ride.

In the job interview, we want to modify this concept just a bit. Rather than passing out business cards, we want to pique their interest while establishing rapport. It does follow a specific formula:

First 10-20 Seconds: Who are you

Start with a brief summary of who you are and what you do. Using your years of experience, specific work background, or education helps.

Next 20-40 Seconds: RELEVANT focal point

Use ONLY ONE of these four focal points to make a memorable and relevant answer.

Key Achievment from my Last Job:	
In the Past, I was Known For:	
I Just Finished:	
My Carer Goal Is:	

**The only exception *would possibly be piggy-backing the "I just finished..." with "My career goal..." For example, a new college graduate who speaks about his degree and then emphasizes his plans for his career.*

Here is a complete example based on my own history and using the Key Achievement focal point:

As you know, my name is Donna Shannon, and I am a professional career coach. I have been helping people with their job searching skills since 2004. One of my key achievements consisted of a contract position that I held for the State of Colorado. I was part of a small team who was redesigning their job searching workshops for people receiving food assistance. Over the course of the summer of 2012, I taught over 1,000 people more effective methods of finding a job."

Notice how much more impactful your introduction will be when you use quantifiable metrics to define the scope of your work. An introduction doesn't need to be long to make a strong impression.

Write out and practice your introduction. While you're still trying to determine your best elevator speech, brainstorm possible answers for each of the focal points. The more writing you do, the closer you move to the truth about yourself.

"What is your greatest weakness?"

The common advice for this question is to "take a weakness and make it strength." This example shows the theory in action:

"I tend to take on a lot of things, but I keep detailed checklists to get everything done. So, even though I may have trouble saying no, I am always sure to handle everything on my list. That, and I know how to prioritize, so, even though I take on a lot, I always hit my deadlines. So, that is why my greatest weakness is saying no, but it doesn't really hold me back because I can always adjust my schedules and workload to hit the right deadlines..."

This answer is an example of "tap-dancing." Under the stress of the interview, candidates start to ramble, trying to bring the negative trait around to a positive spin. This sounds exactly like what it is – a bunch of malarkey. It is not a position of strength; it comes across as a verbal dodge and interviewers hate it. The only thing worse is "uh, I can't think of any weaknesses."

Every career has a typical greatest weakness, and experienced interviewers expect those answers. What they really want to know is *how you handle* your weaknesses.

For example, wonderful salesmen frequently dislike paperwork because they are focused on people skills, not administrative functions. Good administrative assistants have trouble saying "no" to extra projects because they are, by nature, supportive team players. Accountants tend to be perfectionist because they need to be thorough and exact in their work.

The strongest way to answer this question is to be honest about your weakness. This shows introspection and personal understanding. What is most important is <u>how you manage</u> this weakness. That is what the interviewer really wants to know, not some trumped-up statement that tries to turn that fault into an asset.

CAUTION: while interviewers want an honest answer, don't give them a **fatal flaw**. A fatal flaw is anything that would immediately take you out of the running for the job. For example, an executive assistant who is not organized, or a salesman who hates meeting new people.

Think of areas you need to improve. Are you more of a people person, a process person, or a results person? If you understand your own work and communication styles, you can easily identify the weaknesses as well as the strengths.

Answers interviewers hate:
"I can't think of any;" tap dancing to "turn a weakness into strength."

What is your greatest weakness?

"Where do you see yourself in five years?"

The "five-year plan" question is a traditional question, but the right response has changed. In corporate America 30 years ago, the appropriate answer would be to get in with a company, steadily moving up the ladder and establishing a long-term career with one employer. It was common and desirable to stay with one employer for 10, 20, or even 30 years.

However, during the recession in the 1980s, this employment model was shattered by the employers. Rather than reward longevity, companies would lay off the most experienced workers to hire cheaper, entry-level employees. They stopped investing in their workforce training, because it was so much easier to get someone who already had those skills. What was once a 20-year long job turned into 5 years, if the new hire was lucky.

By the time Generation X entered the workforce in the 1990s, work attitudes shifted again. Employees now act like "free agents," changing their work situation to move ahead or to get better salary offers.

Currently, the typical tenure in one job is three years. Indeed, HR now perceives people who stay in one job for more than five years as non-ambitious. The average Generation X worker will change his *career* – not just his job, but his entire *career* – at least three times. Generation Y (aka the Millennials) are even more non-traditional, seeking unique career pathways that capitalize on the changing markets. Building a career through multiple jobs or consulting work is now routine.

Even though we know the world of work has changed, there is only one real answer to this question – and it is the same as 30+ years ago. No employer wants to hear that you will be moving on in two years. Instead, you must emphasize your desire to stay with THIS employer for the long haul. Hence...

The Only Acceptable Answer:

"I see myself working for ABC Company [their name], continuing to add to my skills and making a positive contribution to the company."

If it is appropriate for your role or career path, you can add that you would like to "move up the ladder" with the company as well.

"What kind of person do you find the most difficult to work with?"

If you are like most people, you just screamed "Control freaks and micro-managers!" However, you can't say that in an interview. It brings questions about your ability to work for a demanding person. And, of course, no micromanager thinks that he is one; he just has "high standards."

You need to understand the *why* of control freaks before you can answer this question. Two things drive control freaks: fear and mistrust. They fear being taken advantage of. They fear shoddy results. They fear letting go of their pet projects because someone let them down in the past – that can be a real or an imagined truth. They don't trust others to do something as well as they can, so they create systems to double-check their employees' work.

If control freaks drive you nuts, phrase your answer as "I don't like it when my boss doesn't trust me to do the job the way she trained me. I am always open to suggestions and like to earn her trust by doing the best I can." This satisfies most interviewers because it is insightful and honest, without being threatening or evasive.

If your main issue is other employees, be careful about falling into blame games. Even if a previous co-worker shirked his responsibilities, find a way to stay positive in your statements. Instead of "I hate it when co-workers dump their work on me," try "While I enjoy being a team player and helping out my co-workers, it bothers me when others don't take responsibility for their own workload."

 *NEVER speak badly about a past employer.* No matter what the situation – do not ever complain about a past employer. Anytime you get negative – even if it's not your fault – it looks bad on you. Once you start on a negative path, your attitude and answers spiral downward. Not to mention that you look whiny...

Like the "greatest weakness" question, employers want to know *how you deal with difficult people.* When brainstorming your answers, consider your coping mechanisms as well. Be honest; if you blow off steam by complaining to other employees, this is not a positive outlet. In an interview, you would not mention your negative coping mechanisms. However, you need to be aware of your own tendencies. Re-evaluate your own methods to identify more positive approaches.

Answers interviewers hate:

Complaining or blaming others; "I get along with everybody!"

What type of person do you find most difficult to work with?

"What things frustrate you the most?"

The answers to this question can be people-centered, management-centered or task-centered. Unlike the difficult people question, this question reveals what you don't like to do in your job. Where are your buttons? Is some critical function of the job one of your least favorite things to do? If so, they probably won't hire you.

As with all negative questions, employers want to know *how you deal with the situation*. The best answers revolve around one particular situation and scenario, followed by your solution to the problem. For example, a salesman who is frustrated with paperwork may set up a discipline to fill out the forms with the customer to capture vital information. In this manner, his frustration becomes a tool to stay focused.

When brainstorming these answers, consider all three aspects: people you've worked with, management you've questioned, and duties that drove you nuts. Is there a recurring theme? If so, you might want to be aware of these issues in the job interview. Can you pick up clues from the interviewer about unacceptable situations?

While this exercise may bring many negative responses, guide your final answer around a situation that did have a good outcome or one that encouraged you to grow professionally.

Answers interviewers hate:

Complaining. Creating a list of only negative responses, without mentioning how the issue was handled.

What things frustrate you the most? How do you cope with them?

"What are some past work experiences (or problems) that you would hope to avoid in the future and why?"

It may seem like we've already covered this issue. Not so. While a frustration may be workable, experiences you hope to avoid gives insight into your boundaries, standards and professionalism.

An insightful manager knows what the problems are in her department. She is looking for someone who can solve the problem.

However, some problems are unsolvable. In that case, she needs someone who can work in her environment without getting so discouraged that he quits.

Answers need to be thought out. In addition to identifying the problem, come up with a positive result. The situation may not have been solved, but you should have some professional or personal growth from the situation. For example, sometimes the best answer is to leave a company, without laying blame or acting like a victim.

This question can also be related to the company culture. Once, I was hiring a new administrative assistant. When I asked her about situations she wanted to avoid, she said "I really don't like foul language in the workplace. It is just very unprofessional." Well, at this company, crude language was often the norm. While the candidate's skills and experience were superior, she would have hated this work environment.

Always avoid negative answers or complaining. It doesn't matter if your former boss really was a screaming egomaniac. The moment you focus on bad situations, you attitude starts a downward spiral. This creates a very negative impression with the interviewer. Therefore, you must reconcile your feelings about the past before you can move on.

Answers interviewers hate:

Avoiding the question; victim mentality; complaining or blaming others.

What are some past work experiences (or problems) that you would hope to avoid in the future and why?

"Why should we hire you?"

Some interviewers want to end with a hard-core sales pitch. They are expecting you to present a real strength that sets you apart from everyone else they've interviewed.

I will give you the right answer to this question – it is not your technical skills! Everyone at the interview stage has a similar skill set. Otherwise, they would not have gotten this far in the hiring process. Touch on your abilities, but that's not your final selling point.

It might have something to do with your experience, but even that is not the main factor. If you have unique experience to their industry, highlight this, but there is more to you than just your work history.

What sets you aside from every other candidate is your personality. No one is exactly like you. Determination, professionalism, grace under fire: have you demonstrated these attributes throughout the job interview? Are you helpful and supportive? Did you bring up examples? What is your best trait as an employee? How about as a person?

Your final pitch is a summary of one or two top skills or abilities, plus a reiteration of your unique self. All good presentations follow the same pattern: tell them what you are going to say, tell them, and then remind them of what you just said. Add some of your own self to this. Always remember, employers hire *people, not just skill sets*.

Answers interviewers hate:

Boring repetition of your resume or a lack of preparation.

Why should we hire you?

(*Or the more tactful*) If hired, what could you contribute that the other candidates could not?

Behavioral Interviewing

Without a doubt, behavioral interviews are the most difficult ones. In this case, you are required to think of specific situations from your past and formulate a comprehensive answer, including the final result.

Behavioral interviewing became very popular with recruiters and HR departments around 2008. The whole concept revolves around the thought that your past performance will indicate your future behavior; hence, the heavy emphasis on stories and real-world experiences from your past.

As I touched on briefly at the beginning of this chapter, these situational questions are often predicated with statements like, "Tell me about a time when..." or "Describe a situation where..." THIS is when it is critical to take a quick pause or even repeat part of the question to give your brain a moment to identify an appropriate story and formulate a structured answer.

STAR Stories

Following the STAR acronym is a great way to make sure your stories have a clear beginning, middle, and end that also captures quantified results. Specifically, STAR stands for:

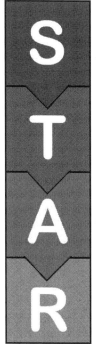

Situation:
A specific, real world example that relates to the question

Task:
Your task, job dutites or responsibilities within that situation

Action:
What you actually did

Result:
The measurable outcome of your action

In practice, it flows like this:

Sample: Tell us about a time when you had to manage a large project.

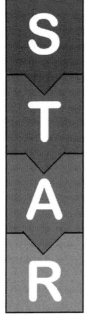

Situation:
Our company was putting on a conference for out employees scattered around the state.

Task:
As the executive assistant, my supervisor tasked me with organizing the event.

Action:
I selected the speakers, found the venue, contracted the caterers and managed the atendee list

Result:
Many of the 500 employees that attended stated it was the most meaningful conference in the past 5 years.

When giving your answer, it is not necessary to say the words Situation, Task, Action, and Result. The pattern is for your internal process to make sure you stay on track and don't ramble.

Now practice writing out your answers with these two sample behavioral questions:

Q: Tell me about a time when you had to deal with a conflict at work:

S

Situation:

_____

_____

T

Task:

_____

_____

A

Action:

_____

_____

R

Result:

_____

_____

_____

_____

_____

_____

_____

Q: Tell me about a decision you made while under a lot of pressure.

S

Situation:

_____

_____

T

Task:

_____

_____

A

Action:

_____

_____

R

Result:

_____

_____

_____

_____

_____

_____

Homework:

Appendix III: Practice Interview Questions contains a list of the "The 100 Worst Interview Questions of All Time." While many of them are behavioral/situational questions, not all of them are. Go through the list carefully and write down your answers to the ones that you know would be most difficult for you.

Notice that you need to *write down your answers*. It is not enough to just read them silently or have a significant other or friend act as your mock interviewer. Writing it down hits a different part of your brain, increasing the likelihood that you will remember the strategies better in a live interview.

NOTE: your goal is NOT to memorize your answers. The whole point is to *train your brain in how to think*. One of the biggest challenges with behavioral interviews is that you never know exactly what they will ask. If you teach your mind flexibility, it will be easier to think on your feet.

 The biggest danger with behavioral interviews is using the same story or situation for multiple different questions. It's an easy trap that many job seekers do to themselves. How is this possible?

Basically, the candidate gets the first situational question and nails it. Their story fits perfectly and they hit all the right notes for the STAR story. As the interview continues, another behavioral question appears. While they might think of a new situation, it is a struggle to stay fresh. Then another situational question is asked. Suddenly, the job seeker feels that the first answer is a good situation for this question too. And so it goes, with the interviewer receiving a rotation of three stories for every behavioral question.

This is horrible! The candidate comes across as having limited experience, as they can't think of new stories that would probably fit the other questions better.

You can avoid this trap in two ways: first, answer as many of the questions in Appendix III as possible. Train that brain!

Second, complete the Interview Preparation Sheet...

Interview Preparation Sheet

For every job interview, fill out an Interview Preparation Sheet and save it with your other documents and research on the company. This should definitely include any new information about the company, especially as it relates to your questions for them.

Interview Preperation and Evaluation

Company Name:

Date:

Interviewer(s) and Roles:

Contact Information:

Key things I learned about this company from my research (products, services, challenges, achievments, competitors, etc:

Potential STAR Stoires/Behavioral Questions
Go through the job description. For each of the responsibilities or duties, write a story or experience that relates to that area. Review their Glassdoor listing as well to find specific questions they asked in the past.

S = Situation, T = Task, A = Action, R = Result
1. Resposibility:
2. Resposibility:
3. Resposibility:
4. Resposibility:
5. Resposibility:
6. Resposibility:

My Questions for The Employer
Be prepared to ask at least 3-5 questions specifically for this job. Questions that relate to your research are most impactful:
1. Question:
2. Question:

Wrap Up
What went well? What should you improve? Which questions do you wish you handled differently?

Next, look at the job description that relates to your upcoming interview. Under the Duties or Responsibilities section, write out a STAR story that exemplifies how you performed this work in the past. Even if you aren't facing a behavioral interview, this is a great way to tie your experience back to this specific job. Write out a story for every single bullet point or stated duty. If it is a technical position, you may want to write some STAR stories that relate to the skills as well.

Once you've written your stories, create specific questions for the company. These are not the same as some of the stock questions that I provided in Chapter 12. This is solely based on your research and what you honestly want to know about the company. There is a good chance that these may be answered by the interviewer throughout the course of the interview, so have a few extras just in case.

Wrap-Up

Once the interview is done, be sure to make some notes. What went well? What should you improve? What did you learn about the company?

Oh, I wish I had said that!

Ever get in your car and think of a dozen better answers to a tough question? Unfortunately, you can't repair the damage you just did, but you can avoid the pitfall in the future. When you get home, write down that tough question and all your possible answers. If nothing else, writing down your possible answers gets that obsession out of your head. You don't need to agonize for days about what you wish you had said.

Before you leave...

Before the interview ends, ask for the job. It's okay; you're allowed to ask for what you want. There should be absolutely no question in the interviewers' minds that you are interested in this job.

Start by asking about their objections. Ask, **"Are there any concerns that would keep**

you from hiring me?" And of course, you will need to answer those objections. Be honest and forthright; don't fall into tap dancing at this point.

Don't forget to ask about their process: "When do you expect to make a decision?" "Do you have more candidates to interview?" These are very legitimate questions at any interview. Asking questions along this line shows your interest in the job. By the way, no matter what date they give for making their decision, add a week to it. Not because they are mean, but because they are busy, and time will slip away from them.

Your manner should show your enthusiasm for the job (even if you don't want it.) You can always turn down an offer for an unacceptable situation, but if you get in the habit of playing the interview game to win, you will have the luxury of choosing to say "no" or "yes."

Close with a strong statement about your desires: "I've really enjoyed learning more about your company, and would love to work with you," is a wonderful, simple statement. You don't need to say anything more. In fact, practice this line with friends and family before your interview to get accustomed to being bold.

Leaving with grace

After your final pitch, it's time to get out of there. Thank everyone for their time and get business cards. Be sure to leave them with one of yours. You can ask when you should follow up with them, but don't press the issue at this point. Goodbyes are a formal process, filled with formalities. Be nice and don't drag it out. Some of the best impressions involve a tactful exit.

Thank you notes

Thank you notes are essential. Believe it or not, but only 10%–15% of job seekers send a thank you note after the interview. Sincerely thanking the interviewer will set you apart.

Your first thank you note should be in the same media as your initial contact. If you have communicated through email, send it that way.

If you began the relationship through LinkedIn, send a note from there. If you didn't have direct contact with the hiring manager before meeting, use their email address from their business card.

Thank you notes need to be sent quickly. Send your electronic thanks as soon as you get back to your computer or your mobile device. However, don't stop there. Use traditional thank you cards as well – yes, hand-written, snail-mailed thank you cards. When they receive your card in the mail several days later, it will remind them of you.

You cannot introduce new material in your thank you note. This is not an opportunity to mention anything that you forgot in the interview. Nor is this a chance for you to answer a question "correctly." If you really blew a question, don't remind the interviewer of your mistake.

In your thank you note, point out two or three strong points that were discussed in the interview. Remind them of your examples. Write about your enthusiasm for the job and the company. If you did really connect with the interviewer, mention the points where you felt in sync. It may even be something not related about the job, such as a commonality from your introduction. You want them to remember you as a person. In your conclusion, stress that you look forward to hearing from them again.

Final words on interviewing

A successful interview will not only leave the interviewer with a positive impression of you but also gives you information about the company as well. Finding a job is about getting the right fit on both sides of the table. When you remember that you have a choice about your next job, you are empowered.

If you get nervous or shy about the whole interview process, practice with someone. Don't just lob friendly questions at each other. Try using the different interview styles. Make sure they use the hated interview questions as well. Dress for the mock interview; do everything as real as possible to test your own abilities. Even better, practice with a group. Using others as an audience teaches you how to manage your nerves, and they can provide feedback as well. Taping yourself during a mock interview can reveal a lot about your own body language and appearance.

One manager I knew preferred to hire people who got nervous during the job interview. In his mind, this showed that the candidate cared about the job. It is true that nervous and introverted people get hired every day.

Prepare yourself, take a deep breath, and mind your manners. You will do just fine.

Chapter 14: Tips to Maintain Your Sanity

JOB SEARCHING SEEMS LIKE THE WORST JOB IN THE WORLD. It's lonely being stuck at home, flipping through online ads and company websites. There is very little feedback from employers. Most can't be bothered to even send a rejection letter. It's demoralizing, stressful, discouraging, and boring all at the same time.

Plus, your boss – yourself – is constantly nagging in your head, undermining your efforts with doubt and impatience. As the time between jobs lengthens, so does the accompanying depression and fear. "What if I don't find a job soon enough? What if I don't find something that will pay me what I'm worth? Maybe I don't deserve that much anyway... Maybe I can't find a job because there is something wrong with me..." The inner critic is ready to jump at any fault or problem, both real and imagined. However, these negative attitudes only have power when we feed into them.

Keep the faith

It's important to keep the faith – belief in yourself, belief in the job market, and belief that the right job is out there, waiting for you.

Consider this: every bit of research is educating you, opening your mind to new possibilities for that perfect job. Every job you apply to hones your tactics and your materials. Every interview is grooming you, allowing you to be polished, professional, and natural when the right job emerges. Do not be discouraged by negative feedback; the universe is training you to ensure your future success.

In times of doubt, look for the subtle reminders all around you. Gratitude for what you do have instead of bitterness about what you lost is pure magic. A grateful heart knows peace and serenity, which translates to confidence and a positive attitude. What benefits have you gained through your job search? Maybe you found an old colleague through LinkedIn. Maybe it is extra time to reconnect with your family and friends. It can even be a break from a highly stressful job. Time in between jobs gives you the opportunity to sort through your feelings about your employment change before joining a new work environment. Sometimes you need to heal before you can move on.

Giving back rejuvenates the spirit. Stretch beyond your confines of the house and volunteer in your community, gaining new contacts and helping others at the same time.

 When faith looks thin, walk away from your computer. Desperately searching through endless websites will not yield positive results. It adds to the gray haze in your mind, leading to dismal outlooks for your future. Take a break, both physically and mentally. Go for a walk or a drive. Changing your scenery makes it easier to change your outlook. The world won't collapse – nor will you miss out on a job opportunity – because you took a mental health moment.

Come back with fresh eyes and pick a different task. Don't keep beating yourself against the metaphorical wall, thinking that sheer force will break through.

If what you are doing is not yielding real results, try new ideas and new tactics. After all, one definition of insanity is doing the same thing over and over, while expecting different results. Save yourself from this problem and try something new.

Answers to common frustrations

Maintaining your sanity requires that you manage your frustrations. Looking for a job is not easy, and unchecked frustrations only add to your anxiety levels. By now, you've already developed some of your own pet peeves about the hiring process, wondering why they would treat candidates this way. Do any of these sound familiar?

1. <u>Why won't they send a rejection letter? I just want to know either way...</u>

    It's cheap to be rude. HR is swamped with hundreds of resumes. Rejection letters are the very bottom of their priority list. Even an automated reply requires updating the database. To help get around this time-consuming task, many companies now use an automated response when you apply to the job, which includes statements like "We will contact you if your skills and experience are appropriate for the position." If you don't hear back from a company within 4–6 weeks, it's safe to assume you didn't make the cut.

2. <u>If a job closes in two weeks, why do they leave the ad on an employment site for two months?</u>

    HR departments get so busy that they forget to take the job down OR...
    They want to keep the field open. If the top candidate falls through, it costs money to re-list the job opening. However, keeping the same posting up costs no extra cash.

3. <u>I interviewed, but I didn't get the job. When I asked for feedback as to why, I only got vague and generalized answers. Why?</u>

    Legal reasons. No company wants to open this can of worms. Hiring decisions are confidential, especially in the litigation-happy attitudes of the American public. If you are working with a professional recruiter, you might get better feedback. However, even this answer will be guarded. This is another reason why it is helpful to work with a job search counselor to gain professional advice and critiques.

4. <u>How can I research blind ads to get directly to the hiring manager?</u>

You can't – that's why they ran a blind ad. However, if you are in touch with your industry and staying on top of the news, you might be able to make an educated guess.

If you can't deduce the company, submit your best cover letter and resume for the situation. While you can't discuss their specific business, use some tricks from this book to stand out from the crowd.

5. <u>Two separate experts reviewed my resume and gave me vastly different opinions. Which one should I believe?</u>

Consider the source. Do they understand your field? Are they looking at the content, or just the format? What is their expertise? All resume reviews are subjective, but for accurate advice, ask someone who understands *the hiring manager's point of view,* not just stock answers or cheeky marketing tactics.

6. <u>I got strong feedback from the interviewers that I had the job, but the company decided to not hire anyone. Why go through the motions?</u>

Their priorities changed, which probably had nothing to do with you. However, if you can convince the potential employer that you will save the company money, make money, or solve critical problems (or all three), the hiring manager or HR person is more likely to champion your cause.

7. <u>Competition is too tough – too many people are looking for work.</u>

Competition is a good thing. It demands that you do your best work. Plus, over 90% of the candidates are going to bomb in the screening process; 75% won't even make it to the third round. Learn from their errors and don't make those mistakes.

8.   <u>I've been looking so long, I feel like I will never get hired. Employers aren't interested in me because I am (*pick one or all*) too old, overqualified, under qualified, been out of work too long, etc....</u>

   If you start buying into these preconceived notions, that is all that you will find. What old negative thought patterns are holding you back? If you can identify the issue, you can develop strategies to overcome them. Instead of thinking that your age is holding you back, highlight the valuable experience that you bring to the table. If you are under qualified, identify the specific skills you need and acquire them, either through formal classes or online options like www.Udemy.com. Suffering from long term unemployment? Combine your strategies by adding to your skills while taking on a volunteer position at a nonprofit to cover the employment gap. Seek solutions instead of problems.

Overcoming frustrations

It is important to acknowledge your frustrations, but don't let them consume you. Focusing on the negative makes it very difficult to affect positive change in your life. Your job search should be a chance to move forward or in a new direction. To do that, you need to let go of the pain.

Managing your motivation and mentality

Part of conducting a healthy job search is recognizing your personal barriers, blocks and boundaries.

Shiny things and other distractions

You will probably have lapses in your discipline. Giving in to distractions every now and then is normal human behavior. However, if every tiny thing that comes along distracts you from the task at hand...

look out. Don't let daytime TV suck away hours of your time with no positive benefit.

If you find yourself wandering around your house every 30 minutes, ask yourself why. Is the job search getting too frustrating? Are you avoiding doing the research necessary to find the jobs? Are you discouraged about the lack of open positions?

 Is there an undercurrent of fear in your job search? Lack of motivation in your hunt can be a warning sign of subconscious avoidance. When the shiny things become overwhelming, do some journal writing. Take 10 minutes and ask yourself, "What am I afraid of?" Be honest – then write down a solution to that fear. Fear of rejection is one of the main stumbling blocks. Keep in mind that every "no" brings you closer to the "yes."

Procrastination is another red flag. Rather than subjecting yourself to more rejection, you start letting distractions divert you from the task at hand. After all, getting the laundry done does have a sense of accomplishment to it, as you can see the tangible results of your work vs. lobbing resumes at the HR black hole.

 Then there is the biggest distraction of all – your own computer or mobile device. I can't tell you how many times I sit down to get to check my email and get sucked into reading the celebrity gossip online for an hour. Or playing with my virtual pets on Facebook. Or texting my husband – okay, he's the one who starts that, but I have to answer, right? Just what is going on here?

For most of us, the computer is our playground as well as our workspace. Just imagine trying to teach 2nd graders math while they are on the jungle gym... chaos, right? The same thing happens when our desire to play clashes with our need to work.

To help manage the playground aspect, set aside specific time to catch up on the fun stuff. It is important to take these mental breaks. For me, I limit my virtual pets to the first 10–15 minutes of my day.

This way, I don't feel guilty when I play, nor do I feel resentful because I didn't get to relax. Give your inner child recess and your work will be more effective.

Desperation

Your worst enemy is desperation. As the months wear on, despair settles in, accompanied by her big sister desperation. Desperation causes you to throw away your standards. Desperation makes you blind to the red flags of intolerable situations. Desperation can creep into your voice during interviews. Desperation leads to bad decisions.

Next thing you know, you apply to jobs that you would never have considered before. An internal dialogue convinces you that you could be successful in a commission-only sales job, or that you would be happy doing the administrative assistant job that is far below your experience and skill set. You persuade yourself that an hour-long commute gives you the "alone time" you need. The inner voice assures you that abandoning your chosen field is the only course of action.

Are you really sincere about these career options? Or is it desperation that turns your head from your goals?

Check your motives. Making a career change is not a bad thing, but a desperate move won't be successful.

 Two horrible things can happen: you can either get the job or not. If you accept a job far below your capabilities, this brings even more personal questioning of your worth. On the other side, not gaining an interview is demoralizing, especially after you dropped your standards. Nothing can be more painful than being rejected for a job below your abilities, especially with a dumbed-down resume.

There is nothing wrong with taking a lower position, but it needs to be a constructive change, not a desperate one. Your resume and cover letter require a specific tactic to get a response from the employers. To convey the right message, you need to believe it first.

Write your new employment goals in an encouraging manner. Accept the change mentally before reaching out to employers.

Acceptance of change leads to developing a positive attitude. In the hiring game, attitude makes the difference between a job offer and a rejection letter.

Get out of the house and give back

The best way to break out of your mental prison is to do something for somebody else. It can be formal volunteer work with a non-profit company, or it can be helping a friend with his garden. It doesn't matter what it is, so long as you get physically moving and interacting with others. Don't treat this as networking, although that might be a side effect. The idea is to do something without selfish motives.

Believe it or not, nothing will protect your sanity better than giving back to your world.

Networking, Support, and Social Groups

 Job search support groups can be a help or a hindrance, depending on the outlook of the group members. Listen to the tone of the group; are they encouraging and hopeful, or is it a hotbed of discontent? Don't stay with a group that engages in negative behaviors, such as sarcasm, biting remarks, or outright attacks of others. Job searching is hard enough without listening to others' negative outlook.

A healthy networking group will do more than share job leads. They encourage each other, share industry news, and provide honest feedback. Some groups bring in guest speakers or experts. Some others may coordinate social activities or organize volunteer efforts.

Don't overlook groups that provide support. This can be a formal support group managed by a mental health facility or a casual get-together of job seekers who want to address all the issues brought about with job searching. Support groups allow people to talk about their real concerns in a safe environment. If you have this safety valve, you will be more likely to speak positively in an interview.

Another key is to join groups just for fun and socialization. The social website www.Meetup.com has literally thousands of groups in your area that meet every week. The whole point is to get together with other people that share a common interest. It is free to join, although some groups charge for their specific activities. What's great is that every interest has its own group. From Star Wars fans to hiking enthusiasts, it is a great way to invigorate your spirit by expanding your horizons.

Keep fun alive

Just because you are looking for work doesn't mean that it is the only thing you do. Set aside time to cut loose. You don't need to spend a lot of money either; in fact, discovering free activities in your town can be part of the fun. Check out community events and free days at your local museum or zoo. Many cities sponsor free community events year 'round. Explore local hiking trails and parks. Even the tourist attractions can give you a new appreciation of your hometown.

Make the most of what you already have. Dust off your board games and invite friends over. If you don't watch your DVDs, sell them on eBay to go buy some more. Even the library lets you rent movies for free. Used bookstores usually let you trade in books for store credit as well. Game Stop and Game Crazy do the same thing for video games.

Think about saving money wherever you go. Clipping coupons can make a big difference. Many restaurants and businesses run coupons all the time. All hail Groupon! A quick website search will reveal deals, either through their own website or through the coupon outlets. Google the business name and "coupons" to reveal great options. And of course, daily deals websites like Groupon.com and Living-Social.com offer 50% off from tons of restaurants and businesses.

Appreciate the abundance around you every day. The good things in life will always be found when they are sought.

Final words on sanity

Your job search is a temporary phase in your life. Done correctly, it can reveal more to you than just a new income source. Job searching can teach you balance, a lesson you can continue in your professional life.

For your own mental health, watch your motives. Are you driven by hope and faith or fear and desperation? Write about it in a private journal; recognizing your feelings in an avenue separate from your job search will keep the doubts out of your professional communications. Throughout your job search, you can affect your attitude. Believe that you are valuable, talented, and effective. When you believe it, the employers will too.

Conclusion - It Can Happen

IN THE QUIET OF YOUR HOUSE, you carefully review your notes about your top target companies. You have them narrowed down to your top three choices. You contacted one of the CEOs through a common LinkedIn group and managed to send him your resume. You are hopeful, but you're still keeping your options open.

The phone rings. Caller ID shows an unfamiliar number, but it is the company's name that makes you gasp. It's your top choice! Your pulse quickens as you answer the phone in a professional manner. Your voice does not waver or betray your anticipation. It is the HR department.

"Our CEO asked me to call you and find out why you are so interested in our company," the HR recruiter says. "Do you have a moment to answer some questions?"

You agree. You are prepared, confident, and relaxed. You recognize her screening questions. The line of conversation confirms what you believed to be the top qualifications for the job. She is impressed and schedules you to come in the following week.

The office is refined and elegant, but everyone is friendly and personable. The receptionist is glad to answer your questions about the company, especially because you show interest in her and her job.

The company lists their charitable donations on the wall of the lobby; you notice one is to an organization where you volunteer. You decide to use a friendly introduction that mentions your common support of the charity.

The CEO's executive assistant leads you to the conference room where you meet with a small panel of decision makers. Their personality styles are different, but you are not rattled by the combined skepticism and conflicting openness. You secretly give thanks that you brought several copies of your resume as they look over your experience once again.

Your answers are clear and confident. Your questions are insightful and relevant. At the end of the interview, the recruiter offers to take you to meet the CEO. Within moments, your rapport is established by your common enthusiasm for the arts – an interest that you already knew from his LinkedIn profile. The conversation is professional and results-driven. Your skills fit the company's needs exactly, and you well practiced in presenting them during the interview.

Now it is only a matter of going through the salary negotiations, background checks, and reference checks to get you started with your dream job.

Did you enjoy that? Good. Because this future can be a reality for you. Keep the faith – it can happen!

Appendix I: Research Resources

These are just a few to get you started on finding suitable companies in your target markets. Not in Denver? Try searching on the internet for similar resources in your area, such as local recruiter associations, chambers of commerce, and so on.

Company Research

The Fortune 500
As an annual list, this is the definitive guide to the top companies across the country. Large corporations frequently use their Fortune 500 rank to define their company. But did you know that you can also sort the list to drill down into segments, such as by state, Top CEOs, and industries.
http://fortune.com/fortune500/list/

Inc. Magazines Annual Top Companies
Similar to Fortune's 500 list, Inc. compiles annual data on companies, however, they create a list for 5,000. Just like the magazine itself, the list places a high value on entrepreneurship and innovation, not just profits or revenue. Their list specifically identifies the fastest-growing private companies in America.
http://www.inc.com/inc5000/list

Denver Business Journal and other local business magazines

If you want to know what is happening in the Denver business scene, you need to subscribe to the Denver Business Journal. Not in Denver? The Business Journals have subsidiaries throughout the US. Just search for your local outlet. Once you subscribe, you not only get access to their online databases and lists, you receive premium news content which is delivered to your email inbox on a daily basis. http://www.bizjournals.com/denver/

Colorado Office of Economic Development and Trade

All states will have some version of the Department of Economic Development. While their purpose is to present facts about the state to make it more attractive to businesses who are considering moving into the area, the is valuable data for any job seeker as well – especially in identifying top industries. https://choosecolorado.com/

Chamber of Commerce

Pretty much every city or area will have a Chamber of Commerce. In Denver, the Denver Metro Chamber is the largest, but several smaller or special interest Chambers exist as the Hispanic Chamber of Commerce. Google to identify the top Chambers in your area. These are good resources for identifying smaller and medium sized businesses, as they will have a listing of all their members on their websites.

Colorado LMI Gateway (Labor Market Indicator)

This website is hosted by the Colorado Department of Labor as a career assessment and labor market information system. It was specifically designed for job seekers, students, case managers, training providers, workforce professionals, and others seeking easily accessible career and labor market information. The system provides fast access to a complete set of labor market research tools in one web site. It was designed to be a comfortable system for everyone, even the person who has little computer experience. Some of the reports include Top 10 Advertised Jobs and Top 10 Employers for the previous month.   Users can also create accounts to save their search

information. Individual services include Career Services, Education Services, Job Seeker Services and Labor Market Services.
https://www.colmigateway.com

The Muse

The Muse lets you do in-depth research on specific companies. Firms pay big bucks to create profiles that include photos and video interviews with employees. The videos are particularly useful. On Trip Advisor's profile, for example, a senior manager discusses the travel site's culture and explains that people who can't maintain a fast pace of work probably won't like working there. The company profiles also include job listings.
https://www.themuse.com/

Glassdoor.com

A free website that has information on companies, their hiring practices and the salary ranges. All information is provided by employees, former employees or job applicants, so take comments with a grain of salt... To access the information, you must share information on one of your past employers (it can be anonymous).
https://www.glassdoor.com/index.htm

Career Exploration and Data

Salary.com

A free resource for discovering current salaries by title, seniority level, education, and ZIP code. The site does allow you to zero in on the specific job titles and job descriptions to make sure you are looking up positions similar to your target jobs.
https://www.salary.com/

PayScale.com

PayScale aims to tell you what you are worth salary-wise and claims to have the largest salary database in the world. To sign up, you take a 5-minute survey and answer questions on topics like your years of experience, academic degrees, current company size and even gender. After you enter your salary, PayScale reveals your percentile rank compared to other people with similar job titles and levels of experience, among other factors. Viewing the full salary report gives an interesting picture for how your salary might change under different scenarios. As a hypothetical example, if you had more experience or worked at a bigger company, your compensation might increase by $20,000.

https://www.payscale.com/

MyNextMove.org and OnetOnline.org

Sponsored by Dept. of Labor, these two sister sites allow people to enter key words, industry and other information to figure out potential new careers. The suggested jobs include the technical skills, personality traits, work environment, typical duties and other key factors that influence the job. The website has an Interest Profiler, which is a set of questions the user answers to get career suggestions. It scores not only interest, but some general personality testing. My Next Move is more user-friendly, while Onet is more technical in their descriptions.

https://www.mynextmove.org/

https://www.onetonline.org/

Websites with Local Job Listings

Most industries have job sites specific to them. For example, www.Dice.com for IT jobs and www.SalesJobs.com for all types of sales positions. A Google search on the terms will quickly reveal the specialty sites - but as with any website, keep an eye out for scams.

1.   LinkedIn: https://www.linkedin.com

In addition to the posted ads, watch your group discussions for the "hidden" jobs.

2.   Jobing: http://www.jobing.com/

In addition to being a local job board, it provides lots of resources for job seekers. It has expanded beyond Colorado and does have a presence in all 50 states.

3.   Indeed: https://www.indeed.com/

Indeed is the most popular employment website, as it is easy and cheap for employers to use. Employers have the option to post their jobs not only to Indeed directly, but up to 100 subsidiary sites. As a search engine, Indeed.com pulls jobs from a variety of websites, including the individual employer's sites. However, sometimes the jobs are not current - be sure to check the original listing or call the employer to make sure the job is still available. Similarly, many scam jobs will spoof an original job posting, so do be careful.

4.   Simply Hired: www.simplyhired.com

Very similar in form and function to Indeed.com. In fact, SimplyHired is now owned by Indeed.

5.   ZipRecruiter: https://www.ziprecruiter.com/

ZipRecruiter was the first major site that let employers post their jobs simultaneously to multiple job boards from a single listing. Job seekers are highly encouraged to post their resumes publicly as recruiters do search through the database. However, there are a lot of scams moving through ZipRecruiter, especially when targeting publicly posted resumes.

6.   Craigslist: www.craigslist.com

Craigslist can be a valuable resource, especially for entry-level jobs. However, it is estimated that up to one half of all jobs on Craigslist are some sort of scam.

7.   Flexjobs: https://www.flexjobs.com/

As an answer to the problem of scam jobs, www.FlexJobs.com verifies the authenticity of the job before allowing the employer to post it. Their site includes a variety of work-from-home, contract work, telecommuting opportunities and part time jobs. However, there is a subscription fee.

8.   Career Builder: https://www.careerbuilder.com/

CareerBuilder is one of the original job boards that came online in the early 2000's. It continues to hold a wide national reach. However, ads are expensive for employers, which is why smaller to mid-size local employers may be more inclined to use the less expensive sites such as Indeed . It is a good resource for temporary or agency jobs, as the agencies get volume discounts on their job postings.

9.   Monster: https://www.monster.com/

One of the original national job boards, and a previous heavy hitter. Very similar to CareerBuilder in usage and jobs available.

10.   USA Jobs: https://www.usajobs.gov/

The main website for Federal jobs.

11.   Facebook: https://www.facebook.com/

More than ever, local businesses are posting their jobs on their Facebook business pages. "Like" the company to get job openings delivered to your news.

12.   The Ladders: https://www.theladders.com/

Excellent site for high-level executive job seekers. You do have to pay a fee to search, post your resume and apply to jobs, but for an executive it's worth it to find the roles and the six-figure salary that you are seeking.

13.   Stack Overflow: https://stackoverflow.com/

Stack is first and foremost a community of millions of programmers who assist each other with technical questions. If you're a novice or an expert coder, Stack is a great problem-solving resource. If you're an engineer, Stack has job listings and profiles of over 13,000 companies.

14.   AngelList: https://angel.co/jobs

Founded in 2010 as a way for startups to find angel investors, Angel-List has expanded to include job postings. It has profiles of more than 55,000 startups, about 22,000 of which currently have openings. An-gelList also offers novel ways to filter a job search, such as companies with female founders or firms founded by Stanford alumni.

15.   Snag A Job: https://www.snagajob.com/

This site specialized in hourly, part-time and entry level positions.

16.   UpWork: https://www.upwork.com/

UpWork lists jobs and projects for freelance professionals. It features more highly skilled roles than a site like TaskRabbit but covers a wide range of jobs, from administrative support to data scientist.

17.   Thumbtack: https://www.thumbtack.com/

Thumbtack is an online service that matches customers with local pro-fessionals. Currently, Thumbtack lists 1,100 types of services in cate-gories such as home, wellness, events, and lessons. Keep in mind that you must pay Thumbtack for credits to bid on these freelance oppor-tunities.

18.   Fiverr: https://www.fiverr.com/

Fiverr is a global online marketplace offering tasks and services, be-ginning at a cost of $5 per job performed, from which it gets its name. The site is primarily used by freelancers who use Fiverr to offer ser-vices to customers worldwide.

Appendix II: Networking Tools and Introductions

Use these tables to track your efforts with your Inner and Outer Networks. Feel free to use these sheets manually or recreate them as tables in Word or Excel.

Inner Network: Champions

Your Champions are the people closest to you who provide not only networking opportunities, but genuine support when times get tough. They truly want you to succeed. They can be that voice of comfort when the job search gets challenging or the ones who help you celebrate your successes.

As will all of our networking contacts, be sure to make notes regarding the times you reach out to them.

My Champions	What They Can do for Me	What I Can do for Them	When Contacted/ Results

Inner Network: Light Connections

Light Connections are people that you already know, but on a less intimate basis, such as acquaintances or friends. This can be past co-workers, past managers, colleagues, fellow alumni, social connections, and even further removed relatives.

My Light Connections	What They Can do for Me	What I Can do for Them	When Contacted/ Results

Outer Network: Quality Time

Your Outer Network consists of people who don't know you yet. Quality time means that you are meeting these Outer Network members in a setting that allows you to get to know them better. This includes smaller networking groups, association meetings, social media, and reaching out to people directly through LinkedIn or email.

Quality Time Source	Contacts Made	Follow-up Needed & Date

Outer Network: Volume Networking

Volume Networking for your Outer Network consists of reaching a large number of people at once. It is all about spreading awareness about who you are. This means everything from large, after-hours events and job fairs to general social media posts, like writing articles or sharing blogs on LinkedIn.

Volume Networking Source	How to Engage (Articles, Events, etc.)	Follow-up Needed & Dates

Sample Networking Introductions

Many times, when you are reaching out to a new contact, you only have one chance to make a strong impression and get the contact to connect with you. Depending on the situation, choose from these samples and modify the LinkedIn message or body of the email to fit your situation.

LinkedIn Introductions

Connecting to a cold lead through LinkedIn

Use this introduction in the first message sent through LinkedIn, usually as an invitation to connect.

> Dear _____,
>
> I noticed that you currently work with _____company. I am in the process of expanding my network and would like to find out more about what you do. Please connect with me on LinkedIn.
>
> Your Name

Connecting with someone after a networking event

After meeting someone in person, be sure to connect with them on LinkedIn to keep the relationship going.

> Dear _____,
>
> I enjoyed meeting you at [---------event or group] I would like to stay in touch with you going forward. Please connect with me on LinkedIn.
>
> Your Name

Connecting to a manager when there is a job opening

Use this when there is an open, posted job at the company.

> Dear _____,
>
> I noticed that you have a job opening for a _____ [job title]. As an experienced ___ [job title], I wanted to reach out to you directly to see if I can help your organization reach the next level. Please

review my LinkedIn profile and let me know if you would like more information.

Your Name

Connecting to HR or a recruiter when there is a job opening

This introduction is done after you have formally applied to a position. Just realize that many HR departments won't respond to a candidate or accept their invitation to connect.

Dear _____,

I was very excited about your job opening for a _____ [job title] and wanted to let you know that I did formally apply through your [LinkedIn ad, your website, or other employment website like Indeed.] Please review my LinkedIn profile and let me know if you would like more information.

Your Name

Following up through LinkedIn: Replying to someone else's request to connect

Once someone has connected with you on LinkedIn, be sure to take it to the next level by following up with that person. Have a clear goal in mind, such as setting up an informational interview for a cold lead or offering to send your resume to the hiring manager. It is in the follow-up messages that the real relationships are built.

Most of the time, people reaching out to you won't customize their greeting. As an open networker, I usually accept these connection requests. However, I always follow up to see what they wanted or to develop the relationship further. If they happen to make a non-business-related request, you can always disconnect or "unfriend" them.

Dear _____,

Thanks for reaching out to me on LinkedIn. Please let me know if I can do anything for you.

Your Name

Email Introductions

Email gives you a lot more space than a character-limited LinkedIn introduction. The key to a successful message lies in the subject line – without a good subject line, the intended recipient probably won't open it.

Emailing someone after a networking event to set up an informational interview

Subject line: Following up from the [group or event].

Dear _____
We recently met at the [Association meeting] last night and I wanted to follow up with you. As I recall, you mentioned that you work at [company]. I did a bit of research on the company and on your LinkedIn profile and I must say that your career has been quite interesting.

As I mentioned in our conversation, I am working on transitioning into my next role by reaching out to and meeting with my contacts and I would greatly appreciate a chance to speak with you either over the phone or in person.

Please understand that I do not expect you to have a job for me; I would simply like to talk to you about your own career and how you achieved your current role. Please feel free to check out my LinkedIn profile at [URL].

I would very much like to connect with you for 10–15 minutes sometime soon. I know your time is valuable and therefore, I will call your office in the next few days to schedule a mutually convenient meeting time. If you like, I could also send you my resume and a list of questions to make our discussion as efficient as possible. Thank you very much for your time, [their name].

Sincerly,
Your Name

Emailing a shared connection

Subject Line: ___Name suggested I contact you

Dear _____,

Our mutual connection, [_____ name], passed on your contact information to me. As a fellow professional in the _____ industry, I am looking to expand my network to help us all become better connected.

In reviewing your LinkedIn profile, I noticed that we have many similarities. For example, we both have a passion for _____, as seen in our similar career and educational pursuits. [go into the similarities...] Most recently, I have been _____. Currently, I am seeking a new role as a _____.

Please understand that I do not expect you to have a job for me. I would simply like to gather your feedback on potential opportunities and get your perspective on where my experience, skill set, talent, and career goals might fit in.

I would very much like to speak with you for 15–20 minutes sometime in the next couple of days. I know your time is valuable and, therefore, I will call your office in the next few days to schedule a mutually convenient meeting time. If you like, I could also send you my resume and my LinkedIn profile to make our discussion as efficient as possible.

Sincerely,
Your Name

Emailing a hiring manager for a posted job

Contacting managers directly is the best thing you can do for your job search. Regardless of the position, address their specific needs and how you can help them reach their goals, especially in terms of making money, saving money, or solving problems. Because these emails are essentially your cover letter, it is acceptable to use the body of your cover letter as the actual email itself.

Subject Line: Your need for a well-qualified [___name of job]

Dear _____,

I recently discovered your posting for a _____name of job on ____ where you saw it. While I already applied through the HR department, I wanted to send you my resume directly, as I feel that I am an excellent match for your job.

As you will see in my resume, my recent accomplishments [or skills, experience, or education] reflect your needs exactly. [Choose 3 -4 bullet points from your resume that relate to the job description.]

- Key point one

- Key point two

- Key point three

Beyond this, I understand that you need someone who can help you _____ [a big thing that you can help with, as you found in your research. For example, increase sales, reduce costs, or overcome a current challenge.] Thanks to my proven abilities and knowledge about ____company name, I know I can help you accomplish these goals.

I would be happy to discuss my experience and talents with you. I can easily be reached at _____phone and email address. I look forward to hearing from you.

Sincerely,
Your Name

Appendix III: Practice Interview Questions

The Top 8

These are the most common interview questions. For these, be sure that you have a fully prepared answer, even going so far as to memorize your responses.

- Tell me about yourself....

- What did you like most about your last job? How about the least?

- Why did you leave your last job?

- Tell me about a time when you had to deal with a conflict at work...

- What is your greatest accomplishment?

- What is your greatest weakness?

- Do you have any questions for me?

- Why should we hire you?

The 100 Worst Interview Questions of All Time

Think you are prepared for your next interview? Check out this list of some of the most challenging job interview questions ever written... Yes, there are worse things than "what is your greatest weakness!"

Your Homework: Go through this list and circle the questions that would be most difficult for you. Write out your answers. Note – it's important to actually write down or type your answers, versus reading them with a partner or just reviewing the list. Don't worry about trying to memorize all your answers. That's not actually possible. Instead, this exercise is designed to train your brain in how to think. The more questions you ask, the better. Once you are in a live interview situation, you will find that your answers will come more easily, regardless of how nervous you may be.

General

- Tell me about a recurring problem in your current/last job that you wanted to resolve but didn't.

- What kind of environment are you most comfortable in?

- Why do you want to work here?

- Tell me about your understanding of the job you are applying for.

- I see you didn't work from _____ to _____. Can you explain the gap in employment to me?

- How long have you worked at your present job? Why are you leaving?

- What kind of work environment do you function best in?

- What are your salary requirements?

- Have you ever been terminated or asked to resign?

- You said you were laid off. How many other employees were laid off?

Reasons for Changing Jobs

- What are the most important considerations to you in accepting a new job?

- If you joined our company, when would you expect a promotion?

- What is your reason for your decision to make a job change at this time?

Achievements

- Describe an achievement that you are very proud of and was very difficult to accomplish.

- In a work-related experience, what are you proud of?

- Last year you increased sales by _____%. How did you achieve that?

- Describe the most significant project you've ever completed.

- In your opinion, what does it take to be a "success"?

Analytical & Cognitive

- What kinds of problems are you best at solving?

- What steps do you take to solve a problem?

- Give me an example of a time in which you had to use your fact-finding skills to gain information for solving a problem – then tell me how you analyzed the information to come to a decision.

- Tell me about several unconventional methods you have used to solve problems.

- What aspects of your past or current work have been the most challenging for you? Why?

- Give me an everyday problem you had at your last job. How did you solve it?

Insight & Judgment

- What is the biggest error in judgment you have made in your current/previous job? Why did you make it? How did you correct the problem?

- Describe for me the process you use to make decisions.

Decision Making

- Over what kinds of decisions did you have authority at your last job? Which type required managerial approval?

- How long does it typically take you to make a decision?

- What kinds of decisions are the most difficult for you to make and why?

- Give me two examples of decisions you had to make on your last job. How do you feel about the outcome?

- Give me an example of a decision you had to make quickly or under pressure. How did you approach it and how did it work out?

- How do you assemble relevant data to make decisions? How do you know you have enough data?

- At which point do you find it necessary to bring others into your decision-making process? Why?

Scheduling & Organization

1. What did you do to prepare for this interview?

- Describe a project you recently ran. How did you organize the project?

- How would you improve on the process you used?

- How do you like to see a staff meeting run?

- Describe a busy day at your last job. How did you organize your day?

- How do you keep track of your own paperwork, schedules, etc.? Please be specific.

- If you could change one thing that is inefficient at your current job, what would it be?

- How do you assess priorities? How do you then assign them?

- Which type of day have you preferred to work with – a set day, one that is planned, or a day you create for yourself? Why?

- Describe the pace at which you usually work and what circumstances change that pace.

- Describe a time when you had to prioritize multiple projects. What were the projects and how were they prioritized?

Interpersonal Relations

- What levels of management did you interact with in your last job? What did you provide for them?

- What does customer service mean to you? Describe a time you feel you provided excellent customer service.

- Tell me about a time when you became "unwound" while dealing with coworkers. What tried your patience or caused your anger?

- Give me an example of the most irrational, rude or intimidating customer you've ever had. How did you handle the situation? How could you have handled it better? How did your boss rate your performance in that situation?

- Give me an example of a time when you couldn't provide a service that your customer wanted. How did you handle it? What was the outcome?

- How do you get to know your customer's needs?

- You mentioned you left your most recent position because of a conflict with your supervisor. What was the reason for the conflict and what caused you to make the decision to leave?

- Can you describe the person or people you got along with best at your previous company?

Interaction with Co-Workers

- If a co-worker needed help in solving a problem, but you did not have the time to help, what would you suggest?

- To whom did you turn for help the last time you had a major problem and why did you choose that person?

- How do you get cooperation from someone in another department?

- Tell me about a time when you and your boss disagreed but you still found a way to get your point across. What happened?

- Tell me about a time when you followed a company policy even though you didn't agree with it.

- What's a pet peeve you have had about an organization or an environment you've worked in?

- What's the hardest directive you've had to follow from your company? Why? What did you do?

- What kind of criticism have you been given by your managers? How much is appropriate?

- Give me an example of a time you had to take the lead with your work group to get a task done.

Creativity

- Give me an example of your creativity.

- If there were one thing you could change in your current work, what would it be?

- What is a creative idea or change you've successfully put to work in a recent assignment?

Autonomy

- Describe the ideal boss.

- Describe the amount of direction/guidance you need from your boss.

- Describe your working relationship with your boss.

- What proactive steps did you take to increase the output of your position?

- How does your position relate to the overall goals of the company?

- How have you had to reinvent or redefine your job to meet your company's changing needs?

- Give me an example of a complex assignment you have accomplished on your own. How did you get started on it? Why did you set it up that way?

- How much information do you need to get started on a new project or assignment?

- What sort of directions do you want from a supervisor or someone who delegates work to you? Do you like detailed instructions, or would you rather just know the highlights? Do you want them in writing?

- Describe a situation in which you needed to analyze the data before acting.

- What are your overall career goals? How are you working to achieve them?

- What ways have you found to make your job easier or more interesting?

Leadership and Team Building

- What do you do to encourage others to do their best?

- How do you attempt to persuade others to your way of thinking?

- How would people who work with you describe you?

- Give me your definition of a team.

- You mentioned you like working on a team. Why and what do you like about it?

- Compare your last 2 supervisors. Under which were you the most productive and why?

- Who were the best co-workers you've worked with? Why do you think they were the best? What did they do or not do?

- What have been your least successful relationships at work? What did you do to try to create a better relationship?

Self-Starter

- What kind of hours do you typically work?

- What motivates you to put forth your best effort?

- Describe a time you went above and beyond to get a job done.

- Tell me about a time when you reached out for additional responsibility.

- Give an example of a time when you felt it was necessary to be assertive to get what you felt you deserved or needed from your manager.

- Give me an example of a project you were responsible for starting. What did you do? How did it work out?

Ability to Handle Stress

- Tell me about an experience in which you had a limited amount of time to make a difficult decision.

- Tell me about a time when you had to make an unpopular decision.

- How do you handle the need to juggle priorities or projects? What have you done to accomplish this?

- What have you done on, or off, the job to alleviate stress?

- In a past job, what created stress for you? Tough deadline? Juggling priorities? Meeting the expectations of others? Why?

- What have you found to be the most effective way to avoid "burnout"? How did you discover it?

- What happens to your work when you begin feeling pressured? Does stress affect your work?

Ability to Set Priorities

- What do you do when priorities change quickly? Give me an example of when this happened.

- How would you communicate priority projects to others without making them feel overwhelmed?

- How would you grade your ability to predict needs before they arise?

- Would you rather be able to predict the work coming in, or would you rather just "take it as it comes?"

- What system for prioritizing your work do you think works best?

- Have you ever had a situation when several people gave you assignments – all due very soon? How did you decide the order in which to do them? Was that a successful approach to take?

Work Ethic

- How have you demonstrated your loyalty to your current organization?

- Describe a mistake you made or a project that failed and what you learned from it.

- What is the most difficult work situation you have ever faced? How did you handle it?

- What areas in your last performance review did your boss suggest you needed to improve?

- What would your last supervisor or manager say about your attendance or punctuality?

- Would your manager tell me you were dependable? How did you demonstrate the dependability?

- If we hired you, what is it that we could count on you for, without fail?

- When do you feel it is necessary to work overtime? Please give me examples from recent jobs.

- What is an example of something you've done that showed your most excellent performance? Be specific.

- In your last jobs, what obstacles have you had to overcome to get to work on time?

Motivation

- What could potentially interfere with your effectiveness?

- Give me an example of something you've done that demonstrates your willingness to work hard.

- How have you benefited from the work you did with your last company?

- What were the most enjoyable aspects of your last job?

- In all your jobs, which gave the most meaningful experiences? Why?

- What do you need from an organization to feel motivated?

- What is your definition of success? How are you measuring up? How will you go about achieving that goal?

- Have you ever worked for or with someone who was highly motivated? How are you like that person?

- When has your morale been the highest at work? Why?

- What has made you feel excited about coming to work? When have you felt "down" or unfulfilled by a job?

Verbal & Written Communication

- Describe "good communication."

- Tell me about a time when you caused a breakdown in communication.

- How would you describe yourself as a communicator?

- What are you doing to improve your listening skills?

- What have you done to improve your verbal communication skills?

- Give me examples of documents, letters, reports, memos and newsletters that you have created.

- What is the role of written communication on the job?

- How do you go about editing your work?

- How much writing have you done?

- Give me an example of the kind of thing you have had to keep confidential. When was it most difficult to keep that confidence?

- What kind of performance feedback do you want and how often would you like it?

- Give me an example of the kind of co-worker (manager, customer, etc.) with whom you find difficult to talk.

- How much of your personal life do you typically share with others at work? Where do you draw the line?

- Which problems do you feel are appropriate to bring to your manager?

- Give me an example of a time when you approached a manager with a problem.

Skill Base

- What are your strongest areas of expertise? Explain.

- What unique talent do you offer? How did you develop this talent?

- How can you best contribute to our organization?

- What aspects of your job do you consider most crucial? Why?

ABOUT THE AUTHOR

Donna Shannon, career coach, speaker and President of the Personal Touch Career Services, has been empowering business professionals with high quality classes and coaching programs since 2004. With over eight years of experience in Human Resources and Recruiting, Ms. Shannon knows the tactics that get past the HR department's screening process and impresses the hiring managers. Donna has presented at national conferences in Denver, Dallas, Los Angeles, San Francisco, San Diego, and Orlando. The Personal Touch Career Services is Denver's top-rated resume and career coaching service on Google+, with over 70 5-Star reviews.

Made in the USA
Columbia, SC
22 May 2019